RUSSELL HOBBS AIR FRYER
COOKBOOK FOR BEGINNERS

1001-Day Easy Air Fryer Recipes For Quick & Easy Air Fried Homemade Meals

Copyright©2023 Andrew Waters
All rights reserved. No part of this book may be reproduced or used in any manner without the prior written permission of the copyright owner, except for the use of brief quotations in a book review.
First paperback edition May 2023.
Printed by Amazon in the USA.

Disclaimer : Although the author and publisher have made every effort to ensure that the information in this book was correct at press time, the author and publisher do not assume and hereby disclaim any liability to any party for any loss, damage, or disruption caused by errors or omissions, whether such errors or omissions result from negligence, accident, or any other cause. this book is not intended as a substitute for the medical advice of physicians.

CONTENTS

INTRODUCTION 6

DESSERTS RECIPES 11

Air Fryer Oreo 11
Vortex Roast Apricots 11
Homemade Strawberry Twists 11
How To Make Apple Pie Bombs 11
4-ingredient Air Fryer Cookies 12
Cherry Hand Pies 12
St Patrick's Day Chocolate Cupcakes 13
Air Fryer Apples 14
Halloween Cupcakes 14
Air Fryer Oatmeal Cookies 15
Air-fryer Apple Fritters 15
Air Fried Marshmallow Peeps 16
Air Fryer Crab Cakes 16
Cinnamon Apple Oatmeal Dog Treats ... 17
Air Fryer Caramelized Bananas 17
Air Fryer Apple Chips 17
Key Lime Pie 18
Frozen Grands Biscuits In Air Fryer 18
Air Fryer Apple Pie Bombs 19
Blueberry "pop Tarts" 19
Red Velvet Cake Parfaits 20
Air Fryer Chocolate Croissants 20
Peanut Butter Oat Protein Cookies 21
Shrunken Apple Punch 21

SNACKS & APPETIZERS RECIPES 22

Homemade Chips 22
Air Fryer Zucchini Fries 22
Roasted Garlic Green Beans 23
Air Fryer Turnip Fries 23
Air Fryer Green Beans 23
Air Fryer Baked Sweet Potato 23
Air Fryer Ravioli 24
Air Fryer Nachos 24
Air Fryer Frozen Crinkle Cut Fries 24
Air Fryer Pasta Chips 25
Air Fryer Apple Chips—an Easy Snack ... 25
Air Fryer Tortilla Chips 26
Air Fryer Puffed Butter Beans 26
Air Fryer Spicy Onion Rings 26
Air Fryer Green Bean Fries 27
Air Fryer Frozen French Fries 28
Air-fryer Cheesy Mozzarella Chips 28
Air Fryer Keto Onion Rings Recipe 28
Air Fryer French Fries 29
Frozen Waffle Fries In The Air Fryer 29
Air-fryer Healthier Veggie Chips 29
Air Fryer Zucchini Chips 30
Air Fryer Sweet Potato Cubes 30
Air Fryer Seasoned French Fries 30

VEGETABLE & & VEGETARIAN RECIPES 31

Quick & Easy Air Fryer Asparagus 31
Air Fryer Tofu 31
Air Fryer Cauliflower Recipe 31
Greek Style Potatoes 32
Air Fryer Stuffed Portobello Mushrooms . 32
Air Fryer Roasted Baby Potatoes 33
Mexican Street Corn 33
Air Fryer Squash Soup 33
Air Fryer Ham And Potato Casserole 34
Hot Cauliflower Wings 34
Moroccan Spiced Carrots 35
Oven Baked Buffalo Cauliflower 35

Crispy Air Fryer Lemon Broccoli 35	Air Fryer Crispy Broccoli With Cheese 37
Air Fryer Fried Pickles 36	Air Fryer Baby Potatoes 38
Air Fryer Cauliflower 'wings' 36	Baked Eggplant Sticks 38
Air Fryer Squash 37	Air Fryer Baked Potato 38
Air Fryer Asparagus 37	Air Fryer Potatoes 39
Air Fryer Vegetables 37	

SALADS & SIDE DISHES RECIPES 40

Cardamom Roasted Beetroot Salad 40	Air Fryer Roasted Garlic 42
Air Fryer Roasted Squash Salad 40	Air Fryer Garlic Knots 42
Air Fryer Pigs In A Blanket 41	Artichoke Wings With Vegan Ranch Dip . 43
Air Fryer Asparagus Salad 41	Air Fryer Sweet Potato Casserole 43
Crispy Parmesan Potato Wedges 42	Air Fryer Diced Potatoes 44

BEEF, PORK & LAMB RECIPES 45

Air Fryer Bacon Wrapped Serranos 45	Air Fryer Meatballs 51
Air Fryer Breaded Pork Chops 45	Air Fryer Bacon Wrapped Jalapeños 51
Air Fryer Cheese Stuffed Meatballs 45	Air Fryer Boneless Pork Chops 52
Air Fryer Chuck Roast 46	Air Fryer Beef & Noodle Stir Fry 52
Air Fryer Gingery Pork Meatballs 46	Air Fryer Brown Sugar Pork Chops 53
Air Fryer Pork Roast 47	Air Fryer Bacon Brussel Sprouts 53
Air Fryer Country Style Ribs 47	Air Fryer Easter Pork Roast 54
Air Fryer Meatball Sub 48	Air Fryer Pork Tenderloin Lettuce Wraps 54
Air Fryer Corn Ribs 48	Air Fryer Bacon Wrapped Dates 55
Air Fryer Pork Chops In 9 Minutes 49	Air Fryer Grilled Ham And Cheese 55
Air Fryer Brown Sugar And Ham 49	Air Fryer Crispy Chilli Beef 56
Air Fryer Pork Tenderloin 50	Air Fryer Bbq Chops 56
Air Fryer Stuffed Peppers 51	

SANDWICHES & BURGERS RECIPES 57

Keto Friendly Game Day Burgers 57	Air Fryer Frozen Burger 59
Air Fryer Hamburgers 57	Air Fryer Chicken Burgers 59
Air Fried Crispy Chicken Sandwiches 57	Greek Lamb Burgers With Eggplant Fries 59
Air Fryer Grilled Cheese Sandwich 58	Air Fryer Biscuit Egg Sandwiches 60
Air Fryer Bacon, Egg And Sandwiches 58	Air Fryer Burgers From Frozen Patties 61

FISH & SEAFOOD RECIPES 62

Air Fryer Tuna Patties 62	Air Fryer Breaded Shrimp 64
Air Fryer Scallops 62	Air Fryer Fish & Chips 64
Frozen Shrimp In The Air Fryer 63	Air-fryer Fish Tacos 65
Fish 'n' Chips 63	Air Fryer Tilapia 66
Air Fryer Blackened Mahi Mahi 64	Air Fryer Lobster Tail 66

Air Fryer Crispy Fish Fillets 67
Air Fryer Salmon And Swiss Chard 67
Air Fryer Shrimp Skewers......................... 68
Air Fryer Shrimp Fajitas 68
Air Fryer Oven Cheesy Scalloped Potatoes 68
Air-fried Beer Battered Fish Tacos 69
Air Fryer Salmon 70
Air Fryer Keto Coconut Shrimp 70
Air-fryer Salmon With Teriyaki Glaze........ 71
Air Fryer Frozen Fish Sticks 71
Air Fryer Calamari 71
Air Fryer Coconut Shrimp 72
Crisp-skinned Air Fryer Salmon............... 72
Air Fryer Bacon Wrapped Scallops........... 73
Air Fryer Honey Mustard Salmon 73
Cajun Air Fryer Fish 74
Haddock Croquettes 74

POULTRY RECIPES 75

Air Fryer Stir Fry 75
Air Fryer Turkey Bacon 75
Air Fryer Fried Chicken 75
Air Fryer Southwest Chicken 76
Air Fryer Chicken Parmesan..................... 76
Air Fryer Turkey Breast 77
Air Fryer Whole Turkey With Gravy......... 77
Air-fryer Southern-style Chicken.............. 78
Frozen Chicken Thighs In The Air Fryer .. 78
Turkey Stuffed Air-fried Peppers.............. 78
Air Fryer Lebanese Chicken..................... 79
Air Fryer Chicken Wings........................... 79
Air Fryer Sesame Chicken........................80
General Tso's Air-fryer Chicken................ 81
Air Fryer Thanksgiving Turkey................. 81
Air Fryer Whole Chicken 82
Air Fryer Boneless Chicken Thighs........... 82
Air Fryer Popcorn Chicken 83
Air Fryer Cornish Hens.............................. 83
Air Fryer Tandoori Turkey Breast 84
Air Fryer Frozen Chicken Strips 84
Air Fryer Chicken Bites............................. 84
Air Fryer 'kfc' Fried Chicken..................... 85
Air Fryer Buffalo Chicken Livers 85
Air Fryer Chicken Legs 86
Butter Chicken... 86
Air-fryer Chicken Tenders 87
Crispy Air Fryer Fried Chicken Breast...... 87
Crispy Sesame Chicken............................88

BREAKFAST & BRUNCH RECIPES 89

Cheese & Veggie Egg Cups 89
Air Fryer Copycat Banana Bread 89
Air Fryer Hard Boiled Eggs........................89
Air Fryer Hash Browns 90
Air Fryer Bacon And Biscuit Bombs 90
Air Fryer Garlic Bread 91
Air Fryer Frozen Burritos 91
Air Fryer French Onion Corn 91
Air Fryer Hash Brown Egg Bites................ 92
Air Fryer Avocado Eggs 92
Air Fryer Pizza Egg Rolls 93
Air Fryer Frozen Hash Brown Patties....... 93
Air Fryer German Pancake Bites 93
Air Fryer "pretzel" Bites & Irish   Cheese . 94
Air Fryer Egg Bites.................................... 94
Air Fryer Zucchini Pizza Bites 95
Air Fryer Baked Oats 95
Air Fryer Soft Boiled Eggs 95
Air Fryer Cauliflower Tacos..................... 96
Air Fryer Pasta Tacos............................... 96
Air Fryer Ham And Swiss Crescent Rolls . 97
Air Fryer Mickey Cinnamon Rolls 97
Air Fryer French Toast Sticks 98
Crispy Spinach Tacos................................98
Air Fryer Lasagna Egg Rolls 99

FAVORITE AIR FRYER RECIPES 100

- 3 Cheese Air Fryer Mini Pizzas 100
- Air Fryer Jalepeno Poppers 100
- Air Fryer Fried Rice 100
- Air Fryer Gnocchi With Pesto Dip 100
- Air Fryer Taco Calzones 101
- Air-fryer White Pizza 101
- Air Fryer Mini Corn Dogs 102
- Air Fryer Pizza 102
- Air Fryer Grilled Cheese 103
- Air Fryer Pita Pizzas 103
- Air Fryer Elote 104
- Air Fryer French Bread Pizzas 104
- Air Fryer Hot Pockets 105
- Air Fryer Nuts And Bolts 105
- Char Siu Dinner 105
- Air Fryer Spaghetti Squash 106
- Air Fryer Tostones 107
- Buttermilk Ranch Dressing 107
- Air Fryer Reheating Leftover Pizza 107
- Air Fryer Sausages 108
- Air Fryer Bratwurst 108
- Air Fryer Corn Dogs 108
- Air Fryer Sausage Rolls 109
- Air Fryer Chili Cheese Dogs 109

INTRODUCTION

An air fryer is a kitchen appliance that allows you to cook foods with hot air instead of oil. It's like having your mini convection oven on your countertop! Air fryers rapidly circulate hot air around the food inside the basket or tray. This creates a crispy exterior while locking in moisture and flavor inside. Unlike deep frying or baking in oil, there's no need for excess oils or fats when using an air fryer, making it a healthier cooking option overall. Using my air fryer has become second nature now that I understand its functionality. With adjustable temperature controls and various settings, including pre-programmed modes for specific foods like chicken wings or French fries – cooking with my air fryer feels effortless and foolproof. Plus, it cooks frozen foods well, and fresh veggies are given a new life thanks to this nifty appliance!

BENEFITS OF USING AN AIR FRYER FOR COOKING CANNED FOODS

HEALTHIER COOKING METHOD

I love using my air fryer for cooking canned foods because it's healthier than deep-frying. Using hot air instead of oil makes the food crispy without adding unnecessary calories and fat. This technique also helps retain more nutrients, making it an excellent option for those who want to eat healthily. I don't have to worry about that greasy feeling after eating fried foods. Air frying canned vegetables like green beans or baked goods like biscuits can be a tasty way to enjoy them without all the added fats from traditional frying methods. For example, when I air fry canned green beans with some seasoning and a touch of oil spray, they come out perfectly crispy on the outside and tender on the inside – just what I'm looking for in a side dish! It's amazing how such simple changes can make our meals healthier while tasting delicious. Overall, using an air fryer as an alternative cooking method is perfect for those who want to cut back on oily or fatty foods but still enjoy satisfying snacks and meals. Learning how to cook canned foods in my air fryer has been fun and rewarding as someone who loves experimenting with different recipes and ingredients.

TIME-SAVING

Using an air fryer to cook canned foods is not only healthier but also a time-saving method.

You can have your favorite canned foods cooked in just minutes with the right temperature and timing settings. Compared to traditional cooking methods such as baking or frying, an air fryer reduces cooking time by about 20-30%. It saves cooking time, and cleanup is faster and easier with an air fryer. Unlike conventional ovens or stovetops that require multiple pots and pans, air fryers typically have one removable basket that's easy to clean. Plus, they don't produce much smoke or odor during cooking, making them ideal for quick meals on busy days.

VERSATILITY IN COOKING DIFFERENT TYPES OF CANNED FOODS

One of the most significant benefits of air frying canned foods is its versatility in cooking different canned foods. You can cook almost anything in a can using an air fryer, from vegetables and meats to baked goods, seafood, snacks, and appetizers. For example, canned green beans are a popular vegetable easily cooked in an air fryer for a healthier alternative to traditional fried green beans.

And if you're looking for something more substantial, try making honey-barbecue chicken wings or spicy tuna cakes using your air fryer. The possibilities are endless when it comes to cooking canned foods in an air fryer. With so many options available, knowing which canned foods work best for air frying and how to prepare them properly before placing them inside the appliance is essential. With these tips and tricks under your belt, you'll be on your way to creating delicious meals with ease!

REDUCED OIL USAGE

One of the most significant benefits of cooking canned foods in an air fryer is the reduced use of oil. Unlike traditional frying methods, you only need a fraction of the oil to achieve crispy and delicious results. This makes it a healthier alternative for those conscious of their calorie intake.

With less oil usage, air frying also minimizes the risk of ingesting harmful substances in heated oils. Compared to deep-frying or sautéing, air frying allows you to cook your favorite canned foods with minimal added fats without compromising taste and texture. By choosing the suitable types of canned foods and coating them lightly with seasoning or batter, you'll have a guilt-free pleasure that will satisfy your cravings without sacrificing your health goals.

CHOOSING THE BEST CANNED FOODS FOR AIR FRYING

When choosing canned foods to air fry, consider the types of vegetables, meats, baked goods, seafood, and snacks that can be fried with reduced oil usage and increased crispiness.

VEGETABLES---I love air frying vegetables because they are healthier and deliver crispy and delicious results. My favorite canned vegetables to cook in the air fryer are green beans and corn, but you can use almost any vegetable you have on hand. Just remember to drain excess liquid before coating them with seasoning or batter. One crucial tip for air frying veggies is not to overcrowd the basket. This ensures that each piece gets evenly cooked and crispy. I also recommend setting the temperature between 375-400°F and cooking for 8-12 minutes, depending on your desired level of crispiness. And if you want an added flavor, try tossing your veggies in a bit of melted butter or oil mixed with herbs or spices before adding them to the basket!

MEATS---Meats can be a delicious addition to your air fryer repertoire. Some great canned meat options include chicken, beef, and pork. Before cooking, drain any excess liquid from the can and pat dry with paper towels. When preparing canned meats for air frying, you can coat them in various seasonings or batter for added flavor and texture. Remember that wet batter should be avoided as it will not cook evenly in the air fryer. Instead, use a dry coating or spices like paprika or garlic powder. By following these tips and experimenting with different recipes, you'll soon discover how versatile your air fryer can be when cooking canned meats!

BAKED GOODS---Baked goods are a delicious addition to any meal and can be made even better using an air fryer. Canned biscuits, cinnamon rolls, and gingerbread bites are just a few examples of baked goods that can be made in the air fryer. The reduced oil usage makes them healthier and creates a crispy outer layer. When preparing canned baked goods for air frying, it's important to coat them with seasoning or batter before cooking. This will help enhance their flavor and create an even crispier texture. Wet batter foods should not be placed in the air fryer since they tend to cook unevenly, while corn dogs should be pre-fried before being air fried for best results. Following these tips and tricks, you can enjoy perfectly cooked canned baked goods straight from your trusty air fryer!

SEAFOOD---I love cooking seafood in my air fryer. It's a healthier alternative to deep frying and cooks the fish to a perfect crisp. My favorite canned seafood to air fry include shrimp, crab cakes, and even tuna patties. Before you air fry your seafood, drain any excess liquid from the can and season it with your preferred spices or batter for extra flavor. Set your air fryer temperature between 350-400 degrees Fahrenheit, depending on the type of fish you're cooking, and cook them for about 5-8 minutes per side until they are crispy on the outside and tender on the inside. Remember not to overcrowd your air fryer basket, which can cause uneven cooking or lead to food sticking together. With these simple tips, you'll be able to enjoy perfectly cooked canned seafood every time!

SNACKS AND APPETIZERS---Don't forget about snacks and appetizers when it comes to air-frying canned foods. Air fryers can create deliciously crispy and healthier versions of favorite crunchy snacks like popcorn or kale chips. For a heartier snack or party appetizer, try air-frying frozen meatballs or chicken wings for a quick cook time and crispy texture. Remember that wet batter foods should be avoided in the air fryer, but a light coating of seasoning or breadcrumbs can add extra flavor to your snack creations. Another great option for snacking is air-fried sweet potato fries. Sweet potatoes are an excellent source of vitamins A and C and are perfect for those seeking a healthier alternative to traditional french fries. Slice the sweet potatoes into thin strips, coat them with oil and seasoning, then pop them into the air fryer until crispy and tender. With these tasty options, your next game-day spread will be a hit!

PREPARING CANNED FOODS FOR AIR FRYING

Before air frying canned foods, it's essential to drain excess liquid from them and coat them with seasoning or batter for added flavor and texture.

Draining Excess Liquid

When preparing canned foods for air frying, one essential step is draining excess liquid. This is because too much liquid can cause steam, making your food come out soggy instead of crispy.

Ensure you use a strainer or colander to drain any excess water while shaking it well to prevent dripping. For best results, it's recommended that you pat dry the canned foods with paper towels after draining off any liquids. Doing this helps remove more moisture from the food and provides a dry surface for seasoning or coating with batter. By draining excess liquid before cooking, your air-fried canned foods will come out deliciously crispy and perfectly cooked inside!

Coating With Seasoning Or Batter

When it comes to air frying canned foods, adding seasoning or batter can make a world of difference in taste and texture. Try coating vegetables like green beans or sliced potatoes with breadcrumbs mixed with your favorite spices for crispy results. Mix cinnamon and sugar and dredge slices of canned pineapple before placing them in the air fryer for a sweeter option. However, it's important to note that wet batter should not be used when cooking canned foods in an air fryer. The high heat from the appliance will cause the batter to blow around inside the basket and cook unevenly. Instead, opt for dry coatings like panko breadcrumbs or crushed cornflakes for that perfect crunch without making a mess.

Setting Up Your Air Fryer For Cooking Canned Foods

To ensure your canned foods are cooked to perfection in your air fryer, it's vital to set up the appliance correctly – this includes selecting the right temperature and time settings and preheating the basket. Read on for more tips and tricks on making the most out of your air fryer when cooking canned foods!

Temperature And Time Settings

When it comes to air frying canned foods, setting the right temperature and time is crucial for a successful outcome. It's always best to refer to the manual that came with your air fryer for guidance. Generally, most air fryers have a temperature range between 200-400°F, and cooking times can vary between 5-25 minutes depending on your cooking. Preheating your air fryer beforehand is also essential, ensuring even cooking and better results. Once preheated, adjust the temperature settings and watch the food cook. It's always helpful to shake or flip your food halfway through cooking time for an evenly cooked result. Remember, every dish has unique temperature requirements, so consult recipe instructions before starting.

Preheating The Air Fryer

Preheating your air fryer ensures that your canned foods cook evenly and crisp. To preheat your air fryer, set the temperature to the recommended level and allow it to heat up for a few minutes before adding your food. It's important not to overcrowd the basket during this process as it can affect the cooking time. Once preheated, place your canned foods in the basket and set the timer according to the recipe or instructions on the packaging. Remember to check on your food halfway through cooking, using tongs or a spatula to flip them over for even cooking. By taking these steps and following our helpful tips, you'll be able to achieve deliciously crispy canned foods cooked in an air fryer every time!

CLEANING YOUR AIR FRYER PROPERLY

Cleaning your air fryer properly is crucial to maintaining its efficiency and prolonging lifespan. This includes removing excess grease and food debris, wiping down the interior and exterior of the appliance, as well as checking and replacing the air filter regularly.

Removing excess grease and food debris

I always make sure to clean my air fryer properly after each use. To remove excess grease and food debris, I use a damp cloth or sponge to wipe down the exterior and interior of the appliance. It's important to be gentle while cleaning to not damage the non-stick coating. Another helpful tip is removing leftover crumbs or debris from the bottom of the basket using a kitchen brush or toothbrush. Add dish soap and water to your cloth or sponge for extra cleaning power if there are stubborn stains. Keeping your air fryer clean and free from buildup will perform better and last longer overall.

Wiping Down the Interior And Exterior Of The Air Fryer

Keeping your air fryer clean is essential to prevent buildup and ensure optimal performance. Wiping down the interior and exterior of the air fryer is crucial in maintaining its longevity.

After each use, allow the appliance to cool before unplugging it and wiping down the inside with a damp cloth. To clean the exterior of your air fryer, wipe it down with a damp cloth or sponge. Avoid using harsh chemicals or abrasive materials that could damage the surface. Regular cleaning will keep your appliance looking new and prevent any unwanted odors from forming while cooking different types of foods. Remember to also check and replace your air filter regularly per manufacturer instructions. This ensures that airflow remains consistent during cooking, resulting in evenly cooked food every time you prepare something delicious in your beloved air fryer!

Checking And Replacing The Air Filter Regularly

A critical aspect of maintaining your air fryer is regularly checking and replacing the air filter. The air filter ensures that your appliance operates properly by preventing dust and other particles from entering the heating element. Over time, the air filter can become dirty, clogged, or damaged, affecting its ability to trap debris effectively. To check the condition of your air filter, gently remove it from its slot at the back of the unit. If you notice any signs of damage or excessive buildup on the filter, it's time to replace it with a new one. Most manufacturers recommend replacing your air filter every three months for optimal performance and longevity of your appliance. By checking and replacing your air filters regularly, you'll enjoy better-tasting foods cooked in a cleaner environment while extending the lifespan of your valuable kitchen gadget.

AIR FRYERS FREQUENTLY ASKED QUESTIONS

Can I put oil in an air fryer? ----- Most recipes only call for about 1 tablespoon of oil, which is best applied with a mister. Fatty foods, like bacon, won't need you to add any oil. Leaner meats, however, will need some oiling to keep them from sticking to the pan.

What shouldn't you put in an Air Fryer? ----- The Air Fryer is one of those kitchen inventions that seem too good to be true. You can cook practically any food in the hot air multi-cooker. However, there are mistakes a lot of us do when handling an air fryer including not preheating your air fryer, not giving the air fryer enough space, overcrowding the air fryer basket, using too little oil, cutting vegetables too small, using wet batters and not washing the air fryer often enough.

Can I use Aluminum Foil or Baking Paper in the Air Fryer? ----- As a general rule, you can use both on the bottom of the air fryer if the basket sits on top. Using aluminum foil or baking paper in the basket technically can be done as long as it's weighed down by the food however it's not recommended because an air fryer works by providing a constant air flow around the cooking cavity.

Should I shake the basket while cooking? ----- Yes, shaking is allowed. A number of foods will stick to the basket if you don't shake it while cooking. Giving it a little shake is specially helpful if you overlap foods, this way the contents of the basket will cook evenly.

What's the first thing I should cook in my new Air Fryer? ----- The most common foods to start with are French Fries, and also Chicken Drumsticks.

What are the disadvantages to cooking in an Air Fryer? ----- The only real disadvantage to cooking in an air fryer is the fact most of the air fryers on the market have small cooking cavities.

What kind of foods can you cook in an Air Fryer? ----- The air fryer is your ticket to healthier fried foods that still taste crispy-crunchy delicious and leaves you with a lot less mess at clean-up time. Whether frozen food or raw meat or reheating leftover food, the hot air multi-cooker does a fantastic job. Having an air fryer means you can go ahead and cook frozen food such as frozen fries, nuggets, fish sticks etc. You can also cook raw meat, for example you can roast chicken or pork in the fryer. And you can certainly roast vegetables and nuts too and let's not forget you can easily bake small items.

Should I pause the Air Fryer when checking on the food? ----- Since you generally only spend a matter of seconds checking, or shaking the food, it is not necessary to pause the air fryer.

Can I open the Air Fryer while cooking? ----- Every Air Fryer is slightly different however going on the premise that heat rises, if your air fryer opens by sliding a basket out from the side or front, then there should be no reason why you can't open the basket for short periods of time.

Should I preheat the Air Fryer? ----- Every Air Fryer manufacturer will have their own recommendations for their particular air fryer. This is also a good idea since many users find that cooking times are more accurate if you preheat first.

Why are my cooking times different? -----Not all Air Fryers are created equal. Air Fryers work by circulating hot air around the food. The internal shape of the Air Fryer and how the air flows, as well as how hot the air is all contribute to how long it takes to cook a food. This is why you should check often and only use temperatures as a guide until you know how your particular Air Fryer cooks.

What are the advantages to cooking in an Air Fryer? ----- Advantages are many, like we said before, we're talking about a healthier form of cooking. Even though your food is fried it won't be dripping with oil. It's less expensive to run. Cooking in an air fryer is very quick. Also, food cooked in an air fryer is generally really tasty simply because the food is crispy on the outside, and juicy and tender on the inside.

DESSERTS RECIPES

Air Fryer Oreo

Servings: 4
Cooking Time: 5 Minutes

Ingredients:
- 8 Oreos or other sandwich cookies
- 1 package Pillsbury Crescents Rolls (or crescent dough sheet)
- Powdered sugar for dusting (optional)

Directions:
1. Spread out crescent dough onto a cutting board or counter.
2. Using your finger, press down into each perforated line so it forms one big sheet. Cut into eighths.
3. Place an Oreo cookie in the center of each of the crescent roll squares and roll each corner up.
4. Bunch up the rest of the crescent roll to make sure it covers the entire Oreo cookie. Do not stretch the crescent roll too thin or it will break.
5. Preheat your air fryer to 320 degrees.
6. Gently place the Air Fried Oreos inside the air fryer in one even row so they do not touch.
7. Cook Oreos for 5-6 minutes until golden brown on the outside.
8. Carefully remove the Air Fryer Oreos from the air fryer and immediately dust them with powdered sugar if desired.

Vortex Roast Apricots

Servings: 4
Cooking Time: 5 Minutes

Ingredients:
- 4 apricots halved pip removed
- 2 Tbsp Butter
- Zest 1 lemon
- 4 Tbsp Brown sugar
- ¼ tsp Cinnamon
- 2 Tbsp Almonds chopped (optional)

Directions:
1. Place ¼ Tbsp of butter in each apricot half.
2. Sprinkle with brown sugar and cinnamon.
3. Top with chopped almonds.
4. Place in the Vortex tray (or Duo Crisp) and set to bake at 180C for 5 mins.
5. Serve with whipped cream, yogurt, on breakfast oats, or with steamed cinnamon buns.

Homemade Strawberry Twists

Ingredients:
- 5 oz date paste
- 1.2 oz freeze-dried strawberries
- 3 scoops collagen peptides (optional)

Directions:
1. Soak dates for at least 30 minutes, up to eight hours. Drain and use a blender or food processor to blend until smooth.
2. Combine date paste, strawberries, and collagen powder (if using) into the food processor or blender.
3. Process the ingredients together until you have a thick fruit paste.
4. Prep your Air Fryer Oven trays with aluminum foil. We recommend poking small holes on edges to ensure that air can circulate.
5. Once you have your batter made, you can pipe it out onto trays.
6. Dehydrate the twists at 125 degrees F for 18-24 hours.
7. Store in an airtight container. Enjoy!

How To Make Apple Pie Bombs In Your Air Fryer

Ingredients:
- ¾ cup granulated sugar
- 3 teaspoons apple pie spice
- 1 can (8 count) Pillsbury Grand biscuits
- 1 cup apple pie filling, with apples cut into small pieces
- 1 teaspoon cinnamon
- 1 stick butter, melted

Directions:
1. In a medium-size bowl, mix the sugar and apple pie spice. Set aside.
2. Remove the biscuits from the can and separate each into two layers. Using a rolling pin, roll each layer of biscuit into a 4-inch circle. (until you are left with 16 circles.)
3. In a small bowl, combine the apple pie filling with cinnamon. Mix to combine.
4. Spoon about 1 tablespoon of the apple pie filling and cinnamon mixture into the center of each circle.
5. Use your fingers to pull sides together and pinch to seal. Roll into balls.
6. Spray the basket of an air fryer with nonstick cooking spray.
7. Working in batches, place the balls into an air fryer basket about 2 inches apart. Spray the tops with cooking spray.
8. Air fry at 350°F for 8-9 minutes, or until golden brown.
9. Carefully remove the balls from the air fryer, dipping or brushing each in melted butter.
10. Roll each dipped apple pie bomb into the apple pie spice and sugar mixture. Repeat with the remaining batches.
11. Serve immediately or at room temperature and enjoy!

4-ingredient Air Fryer Cookies
Servings: 6
Cooking Time: 10 Minutes
Ingredients:
- 100g/3½oz hazelnut chocolate spread
- 75g/2¾oz plain flour
- 3 tbsp full-fat milk
- 40g/1½oz chocolate (any type), melted, to decorate

Directions:
1. Preheat the air fryer to 180C. Place the chocolate spread, flour and milk in a bowl. Mix well and then, using your hands, bring together to make a firm dough.
2. Roll the mixture into 6 evenly sized balls then flatten into cookies. Lay a sheet of baking paper in the air fryer basket then place the cookies on top, leaving a little space between each one.
3. Air fry for 8–10 minutes then carefully lift out. Drizzle over the melted chocolate and leave to cool before serving.

NOTES
If you don't have an air fryer, you can cook these in an oven preheated to 200C/180C Fan/Gas 6 for 12–14 minutes.
You may find the mixture easier to roll if you chill the hazelnut chocolate spread before using. You could also chill the dough in the fridge before baking.
Use plain chocolate spread if you like and decorate them anyway you want to.

Cherry Hand Pies
Servings: 14
Cooking Time: 8 Minutes
Ingredients:
- Cherry Hand Pie:
- 12 ounces frozen or fresh cherries, pitted
- 1 tablespoon lemon juice
- ¼ cup granulated sugar
- A pinch of kosher salt
- 1 tablespoon cornstarch
- ½ teaspoon almond extract
- 2 sheets frozen puff pastry, thawed
- 1 egg, beaten
- Glaze:
- 1 cup powdered sugar
- 1 tablespoon whole milk
- ½ teaspoon vanilla extract
- Items Needed:
- Rolling pin
- 3-inch round cutter
- Baking sheet
- Wax paper

Directions:
1. Combine the cherries, lemon juice, sugar, and salt in a saucepan over medium-high

heat. Bring mixture to a boil, then reduce to a simmer for 5 minutes.
2. Smash some of the cherries lightly with a fork.
3. Place the cornstarch in a small bowl. Add 3 tablespoons of the cherry liquid and stir until no clumps remain.
4. Pour the cornstarch mixture into the saucepan and stir. When the mixture thickens, remove from heat, stir in the almond extract, and refrigerate until slightly chilled.
5. Roll out each puff pastry sheet on a floured surface into a 9 x 12-inch rectangle. Using a 3-inch round cutter, cut out circles in the puff pastry.
6. Place the circles onto a baking sheet lined with wax paper.
7. Spoon about 2 teaspoons of cherry filling onto half of the puff pastry circles. Brush the edges with some of the beaten egg and place the remaining puff pastry circles on top to enclose.
8. Press the edges with a fork to seal. Refrigerate for 20 minutes.
9. Select the Preheat function on the Air Fryer, adjust temperature to 350°F, and press Start/Pause.
10. Cut a 1-inch vent in the top of each pastry. Brush the tops with more of the beaten egg.
11. Place the cherry hand pies into the preheated fryer baskets.
12. Set time to 8 minutes, then press Start/Pause.
13. Remove when golden and puffed. Transfer to a wire rack immediately and allow to cool completely.
14. Whisk the glaze ingredients together in a small bowl until smooth, then glaze the cooled cherry hand pies.
15. Serve the pies when the glaze is set.

St Patrick's Day Air Fryer Oven Chocolate Guinness Cupcakes

Ingredients:
- 2 cups all-purpose flour
- 1 teaspoon baking soda
- 1 teaspoon baking powder
- ¾ teaspoon salt
- 1 cup butter
- 1 cup Guinness stout
- ¾ cup special cocoa powder
- 1 tablespoon instant coffee granules
- 1 ½ cups granulated sugar
- ½ cup packed brown sugar
- 2 teaspoons vanilla
- 3 eggs
- ¾ cup sour cream
- 1 ½ cups butter, softened
- 4 cups powdered sugar
- 6 tablespoons Irish cream liqueur or caramel-flavor coffee creamer
- ⅓ cup caramel sauce
- ½ cup assorted green and/or gold sprinkles

Directions:
1. Line twenty-four 2 1/2-inch muffin cups with cupcake liners. In a large bowl whisk together flour, baking soda, baking powder, and 3/4 teaspoon salt, set aside.
2. In separate bowl, add 1 cup of hot melted butter, add in the room temperature Guinness, cocoa powder, instant coffee, and granulated sugar. Continue stirring until smooth.
3. In the bowl of an electric mixer, or hand held mixer, combine brown sugar and 1 teaspoon of the vanilla. Add melted butter mixture and beat on medium-low until cooled. Add eggs one at a time, beating after each addition until eggs are incorporated.
4. With mixer on medium, combine flour and batter mixtures. Once combined, add the sour cream, beating until combined and scraping down the sides of the bowl as necessary. Divide batter evenly among muffin cups. (They will be nearly full.)

5. Bake at 300 F for about 18 to 25 minutes or until a toothpick inserted in the centers comes out clean. Let cool in pans 5 minutes; remove to wire rack. Let cool.
6. Frosting:
7. For frosting: In the bowl of an electric mixer beat the softened butter on medium-high until creamy. Reduce speed; add powdered sugar, liqueur, caramel sauce, and the remaining 1 teaspoon vanilla. Increase speed to medium-high; beat until frosting is smooth and fluffy.
8. Pipe or frost cupcakes and add sprinkles. Makes 24 cupcakes. Enjoy!

Air Fryer Apples

Servings: 4
Cooking Time: 10 Minutes

Ingredients:
- 4 medium apples
- 1 tablespoon coconut oil
- 1 tablespoon granulated sugar
- 1 teaspoon ground cinnamon
- 1 teaspoon vanilla

Directions:
1. In a small bowl combine oil, sugar, cinnamon and vanilla.
2. Wash and pat apples dry with paper towels. Use a paring knife to peel skin off and cut apples into quarters. Then cut the thin piece of core off of each individual piece. Cut apples again into slices (half-moon shapes).
3. Once the apples are sliced, add apple slices to the bowl mix and lightly toss them in the mixture until all slices are fully coated.
4. Set air fryer to 380 degrees F, Place apples in a single layer a Pyrex, Corning ware, or large ramekin bowl, and place in the air fryer basket. Air fry for 10-15 minutes, until the apples are soft and golden brown.
5. Allow apples to cool for 2-3 minutes and then serve immediately.

NOTES
Optional toppings: A scoop of vanilla ice cream, whipped cream, caramel sauce or vanilla yogurt.

Optional: if you want larger pieces of apple, use apple halves or quarters.
Tips: Cut apple slices approximately the same size so they cook evenly.

Halloween Cupcakes In The Air Fryer Oven

Ingredients:
- Cupcakes:
- 12 tbsp butter
- 1/2 sugar
- 3 eggs
- 2 1/2 vanilla extract
- 1/2 cup sour cream
- 1 cup buttermilk
- 1 cup melted baking chocolate
- 1 3/4 cup all-purpose flour
- 1 1/2 tsp baking soda
- 1/4 tsp salt
- Frosting:
- 12 oz cream cheese
- 1 1/2 tbsp butter
- 1 1/2 cup powdered sugar
- Red and yellow food coloring

Directions:
1. Cake Batter:
2. In a large mixing bowl, add 12 tbsp of butter and 1/2 cup sugar.
3. Beat with a mixer until creamy.
4. Once creamy, beat in three eggs, one at a time.
5. Then, 2 1/2 tsp Vanilla extract and set aside
6. In a medium mixing bowl, whisk together 1/2 cup sour cream and 1 cup buttermilk.
7. In a small mixing bowl, combine 1 cup melted baking chocolate, 1 3/4 all-purpose flour, 1 1/2 tsp baking soda, and 1/4 tsp salt.
8. Now beat together all three ingredients a portion at a time.
9. Fill cupcake wrappers about 2/3 full with the cake batter.
10. Place the cupcakes on the center rack and set the cooking preset to 'Bake' - adjust the temperature to 300° for 5 minutes.
11. After 5 minutes, remove cupcakes, rotate and return to the center rack and bake for

another 5 minutes at 300° using the 'Bake' preset.
12. Frosting:
13. In a medium mixing bowl, beat together 12 oz cream cheese, 1 1/2 sticks butter, and 1 1/2 cup of powder sugar.
14. Add in equal portions red and yellow food coloring - mix well.
15. Once the cupcakes are cool, frost each one using a piping bag and have fun decorating!

Air Fryer Oatmeal Cookies
Servings: 24
Cooking Time: 9 Minutes

Ingredients:
- ½ cup butter softened
- ¼ cup sugar
- ½ cup packed brown sugar
- 1 egg large, room temperature
- ½ teaspoon vanilla
- 1 ½ cups quick-cooking oats
- ¾ cup all-purpose flour + 2 tablespoons
- ½ teaspoon baking soda
- 1 teaspoon salt
- ½ teaspoon cinnamon
- ½ cup chocolate chips
- ½ cup raisins

Directions:
1. Preheat air fryer to 325°F without parchment paper.
2. Cream butter and sugar in a bowl with a hand mixer. Beat in egg and vanilla.
3. Combine oats, flour, baking soda, cinnamon, and salt in a bowl. Add a bit at a time to the egg mixture.
4. Fold in chocolate chips and raisins.
5. Place tablespoons of cookie dough on a small piece of parchment paper in the air fryer basket about 1" apart.
6. Air fry for 6-9 minutes or just until golden on the edges. Repeat with remaining dough, subsequent batches may take 1 minute less.

Notes
For high-rising cookies, avoid overmixing the dough. Chill the dough for 30 minutes before air frying so the cookies spread evenly.

Air-fryer Apple Fritters
Servings: 15
Cooking Time: 10 Minutes

Ingredients:
- 1-1/2 cups all-purpose flour
- 1/4 cup sugar
- 2 teaspoons baking powder
- 1-1/2 teaspoons ground cinnamon
- 1/2 teaspoon salt
- 2/3 cup 2% milk
- 2 large eggs, room temperature
- 1 tablespoon lemon juice
- 1-1/2 teaspoons vanilla extract, divided
- 2 medium Honeycrisp apples, peeled and chopped
- Cooking spray
- BROWNED BUTTER GLAZE:
- 1/4 cup butter
- 1 cup confectioners' sugar
- 1 tablespoon 2% milk

Directions:
1. Preheat air fryer to 410°. In a large bowl, combine flour, sugar, baking powder, cinnamon and salt. Add milk, eggs, lemon juice and 1 teaspoon vanilla extract; stir just until moistened. Fold in apples.
2. Line air-fryer basket with parchment (cut to fit); spritz with cooking spray. In batches, drop dough by 1/4 cupfuls 2 in. apart onto parchment. Spritz with cooking spray. Cook until golden brown, 5-6 minutes. Turn fritters; continue to air-fry until golden brown, 1-2 minutes.
3. Melt butter in small saucepan over medium-high heat. Carefully cook until butter starts to brown and foam, about 5 minutes. Remove from heat; cool slightly. Add confectioners' sugar, 1 tablespoon milk and remaining 1/2 teaspoon vanilla extract to browned butter; whisk until smooth. Drizzle over fritters before serving.

Air Fried Marshmallow Peeps

Servings: 4
Cooking Time: 5 Minutes

Ingredients:
- 1 package Marshmallow Peeps
- 1 Can Crescent Rolls 8 crescent rolls

Directions:
1. To make these peeps, begin by unrolling and separating each crescent roll.
2. Place one peep at the end of the crescent toll and roll until it is completely wrapped. Be sure to pinch any exposed parts of the peep.
3. Spray basket with nonstick cooking spray, or line with air fryer parchment paper. Place wrapped peeps in the prepared basket, leaving a small space in between peeps.
4. Air fry peeps at 350 degrees for about 5 minutes, until crescent rolls are golden brown
5. Carefully remove them from the Air fryer. Sprinkle with powdered sugar, drizzle with chocolate syrup or frosting glaze.

NOTES
I make these in my Cosori 5.8 air fryer. Depending on size and wattage of the air fryer, you may need to add 1-2 additional minutes to cook time.
Leave enough room in between wrapped peeps, allowing room for the roll puff as it cooks.
Do not stack or overlap peeps in the basket. The dough may not cook evenly.
You can make 4 or 8 fried peeps in a batch, depending on what will fit in your basket.

Air Fryer Crab Cakes

Servings: 11-12
Cooking Time: 14 Minutes

Ingredients:
- 12 ounces canned lump crab meat, well drained
- 1/2 cup panko crumbs
- 1/4 cup diced celery
- 1 tablespoon chopped green onion
- 1 tablespoon mayonnaise
- 1 tablespoon extra virgin olive oil
- 1 large egg
- 1 1/2 teaspoons old bay seasoning
- 1/8 teaspoon kosher salt
- 1/8 teaspoon ground black pepper
- Cooking spray

Directions:
1. Add all the ingredients to a large bowl and mix together until well combined. Cover and refrigerate for 30-60 minutes.
2. Portion out 3 tablespoons of the crab mixture and shape into a 1/2-inch thick patty. Repeat with remaining mixture. You should get 11-12 patties.
3. Spray the bottom of the air fryer basket with non-stick cooking spray. Place the patties in the air fryer basket and spray the tops with cooking spray or oil.
4. Air fry at 400F for 12-14 minutes, or until golden brown and crispy on the outside. (Depending on the size of your air fryer, you may need to air fry the crab cakes in two batches).
5. Serve hot and crispy with a squeeze of lemon and tartar sauce or herb dip.

Notes: If your air fryer is a different brand, model and/or size than the one used in this recipe, you may need to adjust the temperature and air frying time slightly. You may also need to air fry the crab cakes in two batches.
For even cooking, don't overcrowd the crab cakes in the air fryer and make sure there is space in between each one.
To ensure the crab cake mixture sticks together, make sure your celery and green onion are finally chopped. Bigger pieces will not bind as well to the other ingredients.
Don't skip the step of refrigerating the crab cake mixture. This helps the cakes stick together and allows the flavours to blend.
Total recipe time includes 30 minutes for the crab cake mixture to sit in the refrigerator.
Be sure to check out the FAQ as well as the tips and substitutions section above the recipe for more detailed advice and suggestions for making this recipe.

Cinnamon Apple Oatmeal Dog Treats

Servings: 40
Cooking Time: 4 Hours

Ingredients:
- 2½ cups quick-cook oats, divided
- 1 cup applesauce (only ingredient should be apples)
- ½ teaspoon cinnamon
- 2 eggs, lightly beaten
- Items Needed
- Food processor or blender

Directions:
1. Place 2 cups of the quick-cook oats in a food processor or blender and pulse until it resembles a coarse flour. Place in a large mixing bowl.
2. Add the remaining oats, applesauce, cinnamon, and eggs and mix until well combined and forms a dough.
3. Divide the mixture into roughly ½-tablespoon-sized portions and place them evenly between the Food Dehydrator trays.
4. Set temperature to 135°F and time to 4 hours, then press Start/Stop.
5. Remove the treats when done and dried but not crispy. Cool completely, then serve to your pet.

Air Fryer Caramelized Bananas

Servings: 4
Cooking Time: 10 Minutes

Ingredients:
- 2 large bananas, peeled and cut into 1/2 inch slices
- 1 tablespoon salted butter, melted
- 1/2 teaspoon vanilla extract
- 1 tablespoon brown sugar
- 1/2 teaspoon ground cinnamon

Directions:
1. Preheat air fryer to 390 degrees F (195 degrees C)
2. Spread out banana slices on a plate. Combine butter and vanilla extract and drizzle over the bananas.
3. Combine brown sugar and cinnamon. Sprinkle half of the sugar mixture over the slices, flip, and sprinkle the remaining sugar over the other side. Make sure both sides are well coated.
4. Spray the air fryer basket with cooking spray or line with a parchment paper.
5. Place banana slices in the air fryer basket in a single layer
6. making sure not to overcrowd or overlap. Cook until golden brown and caramelized to your liking, 7 to 9 minutes. You do not need to flip banana slices over.
7. Remove bananas from the basket, cool slightly, and serve.

Notes
Depending on the size of your air fryer you may need to fry bananas in batches.
Cooking time may vary depending on the size and brand of your air fryer. If you are only have unsalted butter, add a pinch of salt.

Air Fryer Apple Chips

Servings: 1
Cooking Time: 10 Minutes

Ingredients:
- 1 Gala Apple
- 1-1 ½ teaspoon of cinnamon

Directions:
1. Wash and dry your apple.
2. Using a mandolin or a sharp knife, cut your apple into ⅛ inch slices.
3. Lay your apple slices into your air fryer basket. Sprinkle with cinnamon.
4. Place your basket in the air fryer and set the temperature to 360 degrees. Air Fry for 8-12 minutes, flipping at the 5 minute mark. Your smaller slices may come out before the larger slices; you just need to keep an eye on them. Once they are done cooking, let them sit in the basket for 5 minutes (place any you may have taken out back in) this will help them crisp up more.

Key Lime Pie

Servings: 6
Cooking Time: 20 Minutes

Ingredients:
- 6 graham crackers
- 3 tablespoons unsalted butter, melted
- 1 tablespoon granulated sugar
- 4 large egg yolks
- 1 can sweetened condensed milk
- ½ cup key lime juice
- 1/3 cup creme fraiche
- 1 tablespoon lime zest
- 1 teaspoon vanilla extract
- Toppings
- ½ cup heavy whipping cream
- 2 tablespoons powdered sugar
- Items Needed:
- Food processor
- 7-inch springform pan
- Metal rack accessory

Directions:
1. Place the graham crackers in the bowl of a food processor fitted with the blade attachment, then blend until the crackers are broken down into crumbs.
2. Pour the crumbs into a bowl and mix with the granulated sugar and melted butter. Press the mixture into the bottom of a 7-inch springform pan, then freeze for 20 minutes.
3. Whisk the egg yolks until they have turned a light shade of yellow, then whisk in the condensed milk until the mixture is thickened. Gradually whisk in the key lime juice, crème fraiche, lime zest, and vanilla extract.
4. Remove the springform pan from the freezer and pour the pie filling over the crust.
5. Pour 1 ½ cups of water into the inner pot of the pressure cooker and place the metal rack accessory into the pot, then place the springform pan onto the rack.
6. Place the lid onto the pressure cooker and slide the vent switch to Seal.
7. Select the Pressure Cook function and press Keep Warm to disable.
8. Adjust pressure to high and time to 15 minutes, then press Start.
9. Release pressure naturally for 5 minutes by leaving the pressure cooker alone, then slide the vent switch to Vent to quickly release the remaining pressure.
10. Open the lid carefully and lift the rack out of the inner pot, then let the pie cool to room temperature before placing it in the refrigerator to chill for at least 6 hours.
11. Beat the whipped cream and powdered sugar to stiff peaks and reserve for a garnish.
12. Serve the key lime pie cold, cut into wedges, garnished with dollops of whipped cream.

Frozen Grands Biscuits In Air Fryer

Servings: 6
Cooking Time: 22 Minutes

Ingredients:
- 6 Frozen Grands Biscuits
- oil spray
- butter and/or jam, optional

Directions:
1. Spray the air fryer basket or racks with oil to keep the biscuits from sticking. We don't suggest using parchment paper underneath because you want maximum air flow under the biscuits to help them cook all the way though. The parchment paper prevents maximum air flow under the biscuits.
2. Lay biscuits in single layer of air fryer basket or racks. Make sure to space them out so they aren't touching & have room to rise & expand. Cook in batches if needed.
3. Spray the tops of the biscuits to give them a more golden top when they air fry.
4. Air Fry at 330°F/165°C for 10 minutes. Gently wiggle the biscuits to loosen from the baskets. Flip the biscuits over.
5. Continue to Air Fry at 330°F/165°C for another 8-12 minutes, or until golden and cooked through. If they're still slightly doughy in the middle, leave them in the turned-off air fryer for about 2-3 minutes to

continue cooking in the residual heat. Serve with butter or jam if desired.

Air Fryer Apple Pie Bombs
Servings: 6
Cooking Time: 10 Minutes

Ingredients:
- 15 oz Apple Pie Filling
- 12 oz Biscuit dough
- 4 tbsp granulated white sugar
- 1 tsp cinnamon

Directions:
1. Open the biscuit dough and remove the biscuits from the container. Split the biscuits in half and separate dough. Spread them out slightly with your hands or with a rolling pin.
2. Open the apple pie filling and scoop a tablespoon of apple pie filling into the center of each circle. Fold in the sides, and then cover with the other half of the dough, forming a ball.
3. Roll the dough to continue to round out the ball and pinch the seams and then set aside. Continue making the rest of the apple pie bombs.
4. Combine the cinnamon and sugar mixture into a small bowl. Dip each dough ball into the cinnamon sugar mixture.
5. Add parchment paper to the bottom of air fryer basket and add the dough balls on the top, place seam side down in a single layer. Make sure to leave 2 inches in between each one. You may have to cook these in two batches. You can also use cooking spray if you don't have parchment paper.
6. Add the basket to the air fryer and cook on 350 degrees Fahrenheit for 8-10 minutes, turning them about halfway through, and then again for the last minute. Add an additional minute if needed.
7. Remove from the air fryer when they are fully cooked and a nice golden brown.

NOTES

I like to use grand biscuits, but If you don't have a can of store-bought biscuit dough you can use canned crescent rolls or make your own homemade biscuit dough.

Store leftover apple pie bombs in an airtight container in the refrigerator for up to 3 days. To reheat, place into the air fryer and cook at 350 degrees Fahrenheit for 3 minutes, or until heated through.

You can eat these small desserts all by themselves, or serve them fresh with vanilla ice cream and top with brown sugar.

Blueberry "pop Tarts"
Servings: 4

Ingredients:
- 1 pack (320g) Just Roll Short Crust Pastry
- 120g blueberry preserves (strawberry or black current can be substituted)
- 1 tbsp corn flour
- For dusting Plain flour
- For the topping
- 75g icing sugar
- 1 tbsp water
- To top 100's & 1000's, sprinkles or other topping of choice

Directions:
1. Unroll the pastry sheet, lightly sprinkle with flour and cut into 8 even rectangles (9cm X 11cm)
2. Mix preserves and corn flour and drop about 2 tablespoons in the center of 4 of the rectangles and spread, leaving a border around the edge. Place the remaining rectangles over the filling and press down with fingers lightly. Dock the edges all the way around the tart with a fork. You may need to dip the fork into flour if it sticks. Be sure to seal well.
3. Insert Crisper plate in basket and place basket in unit. Preheat unit by selecting BAKE 160°C to 3 minutes. Select START/STOP to begin
4. Once unit has preheated place 2 tarts at a time in unit and close. Select BAKE, set

temperature to 160 °C, and set time for 20 minutes. Select START/STOP to begin. Check after 10 minutes, flip over with tongs and cook 10 more minutes until golden on both sides. Remove and cool
5. Mix icing sugar and water and once tarts are completely cooled drizzle with glaze and sprinkles.

Red Velvet Cake Parfaits
Ingredients:
- 1 Red Velvet Cake Mix
- 1 cup water
- 1/3 cup vegetable oil
- 3 eggs
- For the custard filling:
- 8oz cream cheese, softened
- 1/2 stick butter
- 3/4 cup half and half
- 1 cup powdered sugar
- 1/2 cup sour cream
- 1/4 cup milk
- 1/2 tsp vanilla

Directions:
1. In a mixing bowl, combine cake mix with the water, oil and eggs. Whisk until smooth.
2. Grease an air fryer baking pan and pour the red velvet mix in.
3. Place the baking pan inside the basket of the Steam Air Fryer. Fill the Water Tank with water.
4. Set your Air Fry cook at 350° F for 15 minutes, then press the Mode Button once to set
5. your Steam cook at 212° F for 10 minutes. Press the Mode Button again to select the Combo cooking mode and begin the cooking cycle.
6. Once the cake is finished, set aside to cool.
7. In a mixing bowl, beat together cream cheese, butter, and half and half. Beat until smooth. While continuing to beat, gradually add the powdered sugar. Beat in the sour cream, milk and vanilla. Will resemble a custard consistency.
8. Using a fork, crumble the cake.
9. In the glasses of your choosing, assemble the parfaits by adding the crumbled cake in a 1 inch layer and the custard filling. Repeat the layering process until the glasses are filled.
10. Top with whipped topping, sprinkles or chocolates. Enjoy!

Air Fryer Chocolate Croissants
Servings: 8
Cooking Time: 7 Minutes
Ingredients:
- 1 can Crescent Roll Dough
- 8 mini Chocolate Bars or ½ cup chocolate chips

Directions:
1. Unroll the crescent roll sheet and then dividing into triangles.
2. Place one piece of chocolate, or one tablespoon of chocolate chip, at the end of the crescent roll and roll until into a crescent shape.
3. Spray the air fryer basket or baking sheet with non-stick cooking spray or line basket with parchment paper. Place croissants in the prepared basket, leaving a small space between each pastry.
4. Air fry at 350 degrees Fahrenheit for about 5-7 minutes until crescent rolls are golden brown.
5. Carefully remove filled chocolate crescent rolls from the Air Fryer. Sprinkle each puff pastry with powdered sugar, slices of almonds, drizzle with chocolate syrup or frosting glaze.

NOTES
I make these in my Cosori 5.8 Air Fryer Model. Depending on the size and wattage of the Air Fryer, you may need to add an additional 1-2 minutes to cook time.
Leave enough room between each pastry, allowing room for the roll to puff as it cooks.
Do not stack or overlap in the basket. The dough may not cook evenly.
You can make 4 or 8 in a batch, depending on what will fit in your basket.

Peanut Butter Banana Oat Protein Cookies

Servings: 4
Cooking Time: 20 Minutes

Ingredients:
- 2 medium very ripe bananas
- 1 cup old fashioned oats (or quick oats (check labels for gluten-free))
- 1 scoop vanilla protein powder (I like Orgain)
- 1 large egg (lightly beaten)
- ¼ teaspoon cinnamon
- Pinch kosher salt
- ½ teaspoon vanilla extract
- ¼ cup peanut butter (or nut butter, or seed butter)
- ¼ cup sugar free chocolate chips (such as Lily's)

Directions:
1. Preheat oven to 350 degrees F. Line 2 sheet pans with parchment or silicon baking mats.
2. Move oven racks to the second from top and second from bottom slots.
3. In a medium bowl, mash the bananas.
4. Add the oats, protein powder, egg, cinnamon, salt, vanilla, and peanut butter and chocolate chips and mix with a fork until combined.
5. Scoop ¼ cup of mixture and place on a baking sheet, flatten the top slightly with the back of the measuring cup. Repeat with remaining mixture, adding 4 cookies to each sheet.
6. Bake for 16 to 20 minutes, rotating pans ½ through bake time to allow for even browning.
7. Allow to cool 5 minutes on the pan then transfer to a wire rack to cool completely.

Notes
Store in an airtight container in the refrigerator for up to 4 days. Can be eaten warm, cold, at room temperature or warmed in the microwave for 10 seconds.

Shrunken Apple Punch

Ingredients:
- 6 medium apples
- 1 gallon apple cider
- 4 cinnamon sticks
- 2 lemons
- 2 cups spiced rum/cinnamon whiskey (optional)
- Whole cloves

Directions:
1. Peel the apples and cut in half lengthwise. Scoop out the seeds and core.
2. Carve faces into the rounded side of the apple. Spritz with lemon juice to keep fresh.
3. Place apples face side up in the prepared sheet pan. Press cloves into the eye socket.
4. Bake at 250 for an hour or until the faces start to brown and dehydrate.
5. In a pressure cooker (or on stove top) add apple cider and keep warm.
6. When ready to serve, add the shrunken skulls to the cider.
7. Serve warm with 1 shrunken head.

SNACKS & APPETIZERS RECIPES

Homemade Chips

Servings: 4

Ingredients:
- 500g white potatoes, cut in 6mm thick by 5cm long sticks
- 1/2-3 tbsp vegetable oil
- COOKING MODE
- When entering cooking mode - We will enable your screen to stay 'always on' to avoid any unnecessary interruptions whilst you cook!

Directions:
1. Soak cut potatoes in cold water for 30 minutes to remove excess starch. Drain well, then pat with a paper towel until very dry
2. Place both ingredients into a large mixing bowl; toss to combine. Use at least 1/2 tablespoon oil. For crispier results, use up to 3 tablespoons oil
3. Insert crisper plate in pan and pan in unit. Preheat unit by selecting AIR FRY, setting the temperature to 200°C and setting the time to 3 minutes. Select START/STOP to begin
4. After 3 minutes, place chips on the crisper plate; reinsert pan. Select AIR FRY, set temperature to 200°C and set time to 25 minutes. Select START/STOP to begin
5. After 10 minutes, remove pan from unit and shake chips or toss them with silicone-tipped tongs. Reinsert pan to resume cooking
6. Check chips after 20 minutes. For crispier chips, continue cooking for up to 25 minutes
7. When cooking is complete, serve immediately with your favourite sauce

Air Fryer Zucchini Fries

Servings: 4-6
Cooking Time: 16 Minutes

Ingredients:
- 3 medium or 2 large zucchini
- 2 large eggs, beaten
- 1 ½ cups panko breadcrumbs
- ¾ cup grated Parmesan cheese
- 2 teaspoons Italian seasoning
- ½ cup all-purpose flour
- ½ teaspoon kosher salt
- Black pepper, to taste

Directions:
1. Preheat your air fryer to 370 degrees F. Rinse and dry the zucchini. Trim the ends, then cut each zucchini in half. Slice each piece in half lengthwise, then quarter each in as needed to create skinny "fries". You should get about 24 pieces from each zucchini.
2. In a wide, shallow bowl, whisk eggs. In a separate bowl, combine breadcrumbs, Parmesan, and Italian seasoning. In a third bowl, whisk together the flour, salt, and pepper.
3. Working in batches, dredge zucchini in flour, shaking off the excess. Dip into egg, then roll through the breadcrumb mixture, pressing to coat.
4. Place the coated fries in the basket of the air fryer and spray lightly with cooking spray. Air fry for 8 minutes, then flip and fry an additional 6-8 minutes, until golden brown and tender. Remove and repeat with the remaining fries. Serve with your favorite dipping sauce.

NOTES
HOW TO REHEAT ZUCCHINI FRIES:
Preheat your air fryer to 370 degrees.
Add zucchini fries to the basket and cook for 6-8 minutes or until crispy and heated through.

Roasted Garlic Green Beans

Servings: 4
Cooking Time: 10 Minutes

Ingredients:
- 1 lb. green beans, washed and trimmed
- 1 tablespoon garlic, minced
- 1 tablespoon vegetable oil
- 1 teaspoon sesame oil
- 1 teaspoon Italian seasoning
- 1 teaspoon Worcestershire sauce
- 1 teaspoon balsamic vinegar
- 1 teaspoon soy sauce
- 1/2 teaspoon black pepper (or to taste)

Directions:
1. Preheat oven to 375 F (or preheat air fryer to 350 F).
2. Wash and trim the green beans, then dry them with a paper towel. Place them into a large mixing bowl and add all remaining ingredients. Toss to combine.
3. Roast in the oven: Transfer the green beans onto a quarter sheet baking pan and spread them out evenly. Bake for 15 minutes until tender, but still crunchy.
4. Cook in the air fryer: Transfer the green beans into the air fryer basket and cook at 350 F for 10 minutes until tender, but still crunchy. Shake the basket halfway through cooking.

NOTES
How to store: Store green beans in an airtight container for up to 4 days in the refrigerator. Reheat in a 300F preheated oven or air fryer for 5-10 minutes, until warmed through.
How to use the sauce: The balance of tangy, sour, savoury and sweet flavours in the sauce make it an excellent choice to use for any roasted vegetable such as brussels sprouts, potatoes, butternut squash and more.
How to add toppings: These green beans are delicious just the way they are. You could also add some toppings if you please. Some great options are crushed peanuts or pecans, and crispy bacon.

Air Fryer Turnip Fries

Servings: 4
Cooking Time: 15 Minutes

Ingredients:
- 1 tbs olive oil
- 500g turnips, peeled and sliced into fries
- 1/2 tsp garlic powder
- 1/2 tsp smoked paprika

Directions:
1. Add the turnip fries, olive oil and seasonings to a large bowl and toss well to coat.
2. Place in the air fryer basket and cook for 8 minutes at 200°C, toss and cook for 5 minutes more, until crisp.

Air Fryer Green Beans

Cooking Time: 8 Minutes

Ingredients:
- 1 lb Green beans (trimmed)
- 6 cloves Garlic (minced)
- 1/2 tsp Sea salt
- 1/4 tsp Black pepper
- 2 tbsp Olive oil
- 1 tbsp Lemon juice

Directions:
1. Preheat the air fryer to 375 degrees F (191 degrees C).
2. In a large bowl, combine all the ingredients.
3. Arrange green beans in the air fryer basket, in a single layer.
4. Cook green beans in the air fryer for 7-10 minutes, until tender. Shake the basket halfway through the cook time.

Air Fryer Baked Sweet Potato

Servings: 2
Cooking Time: 45 Minutes

Ingredients:
- 2 medium sweet potatoes (about 6 ounces)

Directions:
1. Poke hole all over with a fork and place in the air fryer, no foil needed.
2. Air fry 370F 35-45 minutes or until soft.
3. Top with your favorite toppings!

Air Fryer Ravioli

Servings: 4-6

Ingredients:
- 2 large eggs
- 2 tbsp. whole milk
- 1 c. Italian bread crumbs
- 1/4 c. grated Parmesan, plus more for serving
- 1/4 tsp. kosher salt
- Freshly ground black pepper
- 1 (20-oz.) package refrigerated ravioli
- Cooking spray
- Pesto or marinara, for serving

Directions:
1. In a shallow bowl, whisk eggs and milk. In another shallow bowl, combine bread crumbs and Parmesan; season with salt and a few grinds of pepper.
2. Working one at a time, dip ravioli into egg mixture, then into bread crumb mixture, pressing to adhere. Dip back into egg mixture. Place on a plate.
3. Lightly coat an air-fryer basket with cooking spray. Working in batches, arrange ravioli in basket, spacing about 1/4" apart; spray with cooking spray. Cook at 400°, flipping halfway through and spraying with cooking spray, until golden and cooked through, about 7 minutes.
4. Arrange ravioli on a platter. Top with more Parmesan. Serve warm with pesto alongside for dipping.

Air Fryer Nachos

Servings: 4
Cooking Time: 1 Minutes

Ingredients:
- 2 cups Green Mountain Gringo® Original Tortilla Strips
- 1/2 cup Green Mountain Gringo® Medium Salsa
- 1/3 cup canned black beans, drained and rinsed
- 1/4 teaspoon lime juice
- 1/2 cup Mexican cheese
- 1 avocado, diced
- 2 green onions, chopped
- Sour cream, for drizzling

Directions:
1. Press a piece of aluminum foil down into your air fryer to form a flat bottom. Make sure the sides go up the air fryer at least 2 inches (so you can safely remove the nachos after heating). Remove foil from air fryer keeping its form.
2. Preheat your air fryer to 370 degrees.
3. Add chips to the aluminum foil then add salsa, black beans, and lime juice on top. Sprinkle cheese across the top of the nachos.
4. Carefully place the nachos inside the air fryer and cook for 1-2 minutes, until cheese is just melted.
5. Remove nachos from the air fryer and top with avocados, green onions, and sour cream.
6. Enjoy immediately.

NOTES
To reheat nachos:
Cook nachos in a preheated air fryer at 320 degrees for 2-3 minutes until warmed thoroughly.
To grill:
Place nachos on grill heated to approximately 350 degrees and cook for 1 minute with the grill closed.
To add ground beef:
Cook 1 quarter pound of ground beef in a pan on medium heat until browned. Drain any liquid, then add 3 teaspoons of taco seasoning and 1 tablespoon of water. Cook for another 1-2 minutes, then add to nachos prior to air frying/grilling.

Air Fryer Frozen Crinkle Cut Fries

Servings: 4
Cooking Time: 12 Minutes

Ingredients:
- 1 lb. (454 g) Frozen crinkle cut fries
- salt , to taste
- black pepper , to taste
- EQUIPMENT

- Air Fryer

Directions:
1. Place the frozen crinkle fries in the air fryer basket and spread out evenly. No oil spray is needed for the fries. It's already been deep fried in oil, so that's enough to air fry.
2. Air Fry at 400°F/205°C for 10-14 minutes. Shake and gently stir about halfway through cooking. If cooking larger batches, or if your fries don't cook evenly, try turning them multiple times on following batches.
3. Want the fries crisper? If needed air fry for an additional 1-3 minutes or until crisped to your liking. Season with salt & pepper, if desired.

NOTES

Air Frying Tips and Notes:
No Oil Necessary. Cook Frozen - Do not thaw first.
Shake or turn if needed. Don't overcrowd the air fryer basket.
Recipe timing is based on a non-preheated air fryer. If cooking in multiple batches of fries back to back, the following batches may cook a little quicker.
Recipes were tested in 3.7 to 6 qt. air fryers. If using a larger air fryer, the fries might cook quicker so adjust cooking time.
Remember to set a timer to shake/flip/toss as directed in recipe.

Air Fryer Pasta Chips

Servings: 6
Cooking Time: 20 Minutes

Ingredients:
- 8 ounces rigatoni pasta or bow tie or penne (I used tortiglioni)
- 1 Tablespoon olive oil
- ¼ cup freshly shredded Parmesan cheese plus extra for garnish if desired
- 1 teaspoon Italian dressing mix or your favorite seasoning mix (or ½ teaspoon oregano and ½ teaspoon garlic powder)
- ¼ teaspoon kosher salt
- ¼ teaspoon freshly ground black pepper
- parsley finely chopped, to garnish, optional

Directions:
1. Cook pasta to al dente according to package directions. Do not overcook. Drain and return to the pot to remove moisture.
2. About 2 minutes before pasta is ready, preheat air fryer to 400°F.
3. Add olive oil, parmesan, and seasoning to the pot of pasta, toss to coat.
4. Add pasta to air fryer basket* and cook for 10-12 minutes**, tossing the basket every 3-4 minutes until they are cooked to desired doneness.
5. Cool for about 3-4 minutes before serving. Garnish with parsley and parmesan if desired. Serve with dip, salsa, or hummus.

Notes
*While a single layer is best (meaning you may need to do batches), tossing the basket every 3-4 minutes works to cook them all at once!
**The "pasta chips" crisp as they cool. If you'd like them to be a bit more crisp after they've cooled, simply pop them back in the air fryer for another couple of minutes.

Air Fryer Apple Chips—an Easy Snack

Ingredients:
- 1 red apple
- 2 tbsp sugar
- 1 tbsp dark brown sugar
- 1 tsp cinnamon
- For a healthier version, try making without the added sugar.

Directions:
1. Thinly slice and core the apple. Using a slicing mandolin is preferred. In a medium bowl, combine sugar and cinnamon. Add apple slices and coat well. Line the air fryer basket with perforated parchment paper to prevent sticking. Spread apple slices evenly inside the basket and air fry at 250°F for 1 hour.

Air Fryer Tortilla Chips

Servings: 4
Cooking Time: 6 Minutes

Ingredients:
- 4 corn tortillas small
- 1 tablespoon olive oil
- 1/2 tsp salt

Directions:
1. Using a pastry brush, or oil spray, brush or spray a light coating of oil onto the tortilla triangles.
2. Use a pizza cutter or sharp knife and cut the tortillas into triangles.
3. Place tortilla wedges into the air fryer basket, laying them in a single layer, without overlap.
4. Sprinkle tortilla pieces with salt or other seasonings you may wish to use.
5. Working in batches, air fry at 350 degrees Fahrenheit for 7-9 minutes, turning the chips halfway through cooking time. Chips will be golden brown and crispy when done.

NOTES

When air frying, remember that the cook time may vary depending on type of air fryer, and size and type of tortilla pieces. If using larger tortillas, cooking time may need to be adjusted by a couple minutes.

Placing the tortilla slices in a single layer helps them to cook evenly and become crispy.

For additional flavors, you can use additional spices and seasonings. A few bolder flavors you can add would be: curry powder, white cheddar popcorn powder, or a light sprinkle of chili powder.

You can also add a simple boost of flavor by adding garlic powder, cinnamon, a dash of lime juice and then season with salt before air frying.

Air Fryer Puffed Butter Beans

Servings: 4
Cooking Time: 15 Minutes

Ingredients:
- 1 (16 ounce) can large butter beans, drained and rinsed
- 1 tablespoon olive oil
- 1 teaspoon salt
- 1 teaspoon freshly ground black pepper
- 1 teaspoon garlic powder
- Optional: preferred seasoning blend

Directions:
1. Stir together butter beans, olive oil, salt, pepper, and garlic powder in a bowl until combined. Spread out in the air fryer basket
2. Preheat an air fryer to 400 degrees F (200 degrees C).
3. Air fry until golden and crispy, tossing halfway through, for 12 to 15 minutes.
4. Sprinkle with additional seasonings to taste if you like. Store in an air-tight container for 3 to 5 days.

Air Fryer Spicy Onion Rings

Servings: 4
Cooking Time: 10 Minutes

Ingredients:
- 2 large sweet onions, sliced 1/2 inch thick
- Batter:
- ⅔ cup buttermilk
- 1 egg
- ¼ cup all-purpose flour
- 1 teaspoon RedHot Chile and Lime Seasoning Blend (such as Frank's®)
- ½ teaspoon adobo all-purpose seasoning (such as Goya®)
- Breading:
- 2 cups panko bread crumbs
- 1 teaspoon adobo all-purpose seasoning (such as Goya®)
- ½ teaspoon RedHot Chile and Lime Seasoning Blend (such as Frank's®)
- olive oil cooking spray
- 1 teaspoon kosher salt, or to taste

Directions:
1. Whisk together buttermilk, egg, flour, chile and lime seasoning, and adobo seasoning for the batter in a shallow bowl. Cover and refrigerate for 30 minutes.

2. Combine panko, adobo seasoning, and chile and lime seasoning in a shallow dish; mix well. Remove batter from the fridge. Dip onion rings first into the batter, then into bread crumb mixture, turning to coat, and gently shake off excess crumbs. Lightly spritz the onion rings with cooking spray on both sides.
3. Preheat the air fryer to 340 degrees F (170 degrees C). Line the air fryer basket with a parchment liner or lightly spray with oil.
4. Place the breaded onion rings into the fryer basket in an even layer, leaving about 1/2-inch space between the slices.
5. Cook until crisp and lightly browned, flipping halfway through, 10 to 12 minutes. You may have to cook in batches, and cooking time may vary depending on the size and brand of your air fryer.
6. Remove from the air fryer, transfer to a baking sheet, sprinkle with kosher salt, and place in a 250 degrees F (120 degrees C) oven to keep warm.

Cook's Notes:
You can find Chile n' Lime seasoning and Adobo seasoning in the Hispanic section of your supermarket. Adobo should be available at most stores, but if Chile n' Lime is not, use all Adobo. Chilling the batter will make the breading adhere better. You may bread the onion rings, cover early in the day, and refrigerate until ready to cook.

Air Fryer Green Bean Fries

Servings: 4
Cooking Time: 5 Minutes

Ingredients:
- 1 pound green beans fresh
- 1 cup Parmesan cheese
- 1 cup panko bread crumbs
- 1 Tablespoon garlic powder
- 2 eggs
- 1/2 cup all purpose flour
- 2 Tablespoons Olive oil spray

Directions:

1. Preheat Air Fryer to 390 degrees Fahrenheit (199 degrees Celcius).
2. Snap the ends off the fresh green beans, then place them into a colander to rinse. Place the green beans on a paper towel and pat dry.
3. Coat the green beans in the all purpose flour.
4. Whisk together the eggs in a small bowl.
5. Mix together parmesan cheese, panko breadcrumbs, and garlic powder in a separate bowl.
6. Dip the green beans into the egg mixture, and then dip the green beans into the panko and cheese mixture.
7. Coat the green beans well. Add the green beans to a cooling rack as you work to finish the remainder of the green beans. Spray the coated beans with a light coating of olive oil.
8. Place the coated green beans in the Air Fryer basket and air fry for 5 minutes or until golden brown.
9. Sprinkle with additional parmesan cheese or fresh lemon juice if desired and serve with your favorite dipping sauce.

NOTES
Arrange your green beans in a single layer: Spreading your green beans out ensures even cooking through the dish.
Cooking spray: You can use olive oil cooking spray, canola oil spray, or avocado oil spray for this recipe.
Coat the green beans well: Use a bit of the breading mix when coating your green beans. The more breading you have, the crispier your green beans will be.
This recipe was made with a basket-style 5.8 qt Cosori Air Fryer. If you're using a different brand, you may have to adjust your cooking time accordingly.

Air Fryer Frozen French Fries

Servings: 4
Cooking Time: 15 Minutes

Ingredients:
- 1 teaspoon oil
- 250 grams frozen french fries (more or less depending on the size of your air fryer and servings you want)
- 1/4 teaspoon seasoning salt

Directions:
1. Preheat air fryer to 400 degrees for 5 minutes.
2. Meanwhile, toss frozen french fries with seasoning salt.
3. Open the air fryer basket and brush with oil (not totally necessary, but ensures the fries will not stick).
4. Place frozen french fries in air fryer basket in a single layer or as close as possible.
5. Cook at 400 degrees F for 15-20 minutes, checking and stirring every 5 minutes, until crispy.

Air-fryer Cheesy Mozzarella Chips

Servings: 6
Cooking Time: 10 Minutes

Ingredients:
- 2 tbs plain flour
- 2 tsp onion powder
- 1/2 tsp garlic salt
- 1/4 tsp ground paprika
- 3 free range eggs
- 1 1/2 cups panko breadcrumbs
- 550g mozzarella
- 5ml olive oil cooking spray
- 1/2 cup basil pesto (to serve)
- 2 sprigs basil, leaves picked (to serve)

Directions:
1. Combine flour, onion powder, garlic salt and paprika in a shallow bowl. Season with pepper. Whisk eggs in a separate shallow bowl. Place breadcrumbs in a separate shallow bowl.
2. Cut mozzarella block in half crossways. Then cut each in half horizontally to form 4 thin pieces. Cut each piece into 5 sticks. Dip mozzarella sticks in flour mixture to coat. Shake off excess. Working in batches, coat mozzarella sticks in egg mixture then in breadcrumbs. Repeat crumbing process to double crumb. Spray the chips with oil after double crumbing.
3. Preheat air fryer to 200°C for 2 minutes. Working in 2 batches, cook mozzarella sticks in air fryer for 4 minutes or until golden. Stand for 2 minutes, then transfer to a board. Top with basil and serve with pesto.

Air Fryer Keto Onion Rings Recipe

Servings: 4
Cooking Time: 16 Minutes

Ingredients:
- 1 large Onion (sliced into rings 1/2 inch thick)
- 3 tbsp Wholesome Yum Coconut Flour
- 1/4 tsp Sea salt
- 2 large Eggs
- 2/3 cup Pork rinds (~1.8 oz)
- 3 tbsp Wholesome Yum Blanched Almond Flour
- 1/2 tsp Paprika
- 1/2 tsp Garlic powder

Directions:
1. Arrange 3 small, shallow bowls in a line:
2. Coconut flour and sea salt, stirred together
3. Eggs, beaten
4. Pork rinds, almond flour, paprika, and garlic powder, stirred together
5. Lightly grease 2 air fryer oven racks or an air fryer basket.
6. Dredge an onion ring in coconut flour. Dip it in the egg, shake off the excess, then place in the pork rind mixture. Scoop extra pork rind mixture over it, so that it's coated on all size. Place into the air fryer rack or basket. Repeat with all the onion rings, placing them in a single layer without

touching. (You may need to cook them in two batches if you don't have 2 air fryer racks.)
7. Preheat the air fryer or air fryer oven to 400 degrees F for 2 to 3 minutes.
8. For an air fryer oven: Place both racks into the air fryer oven. Bake for about 8 minutes, until the top layer is golden. Switch racks and bake for 8 more minutes, until the top layer is golden again.
9. For a regular air fryer: Only half the onion rings will fit into the basket in a single layer. Place the basket into the air fryer. Bake for 16 minutes, until golden. Remove the onion rings, arrange the next batch of uncooked rings, and repeat.

Air Fryer French Fries
Servings: 4
Cooking Time: 25 Minutes

Ingredients:
- 2 russet potatoes
- 1 tablespoon extra virgin olive oil
- 1/8 teaspoon salt

Directions:
1. Fill a medium-sized bowl halfway with cold water
2. Peel potatoes (if desired) and cut them into 1/4 inch slices.
3. As you slice the potatoes, add them into the water to soak
4. Drain potatoes and fill bowl back up. Mix the potatoes around like you're rotating a salad with your hands. Drain again. Repeat 5-6 times until water is clear.
5. Dry off potatoes and bowl with a paper towel
6. Add potatoes back to dry bowl. Add extra virgin olive oil and salt. Mix to combine.
7. Cook french fries at 350 degrees for 10 minutes, then at 400 degrees for 15-18 minutes, shaking the basket every 5 minutes.

Frozen Waffle Fries In The Air Fryer
Servings: 4
Cooking Time: 8 Minutes

Ingredients:
- 1 pound frozen waffle fries (1/2 bag)
- OPTIONAL
- Dipping sauce of choice

Directions:
1. Preheat your air fryer to 400 degrees F.
2. Place a single layer of frozen waffle fries in your air fryer. They can overlap slightly.
3. Cook the fries for 8 to 10 minutes, carefully shaking the basket halfway through cooking.
4. Remove the waffle fries from the air fryer, serve with your favorite dipping sauce, and enjoy!

HOW TO REHEAT WAFFLE FRIES IN THE AIR FRYER:
Preheat your air fryer to 350 degrees.
Place your leftover waffle fries in the air fryer and cook for about 2 minutes, until warmed thoroughly.

Air-fryer Healthier Veggie Chips
Servings: 4
Cooking Time: 1 Hr 30 Minutes

Ingredients:
- 1 large washed white potato, cut into 1mm-thick slices
- 300g beetroot, trimmed, cut into 1mm-thick slices
- 150g carrot, trimmed, cut into 1mm-thick slices
- 1 1/2 tbs Woolworths extra virgin olive oil
- 1 sprig rosemary, leaves picked, finely chopped

Directions:
1. Place potato in a medium bowl and cover with cold water. Stand for 15 minutes to soak. Place beetroot and carrot in separate bowls. Add 2 tsp oil to beetroot and carrot bowls and toss to coat.
2. Preheat air fryer to 180°C for 2 minutes. Working in 4 batches, cook beetroot and

carrot for 15 minutes, shaking basket every few minutes, or until golden and crisp.
3. Drain potatoes, pat dry with a clean tea towel. Transfer to a dry bowl, add remaining oil and toss to coat. Working in 2 batches, cook potato for 15 minutes, shaking basket every few minutes, or until golden and crisp. Sprinkle chips with rosemary to serve.

Air Fryer Zucchini Chips
Servings: 4
Cooking Time: 12 Minutes

Ingredients:
- 1 medium zucchini cut into ½" coins
- 1 beaten egg
- cooking spray
- Crumb Coating
- ⅔ cup Panko bread crumbs
- ⅔ cup seasoned bread crumbs
- 2 tablespoons Parmesan cheese grated
- 1 teaspoon Italian seasoning

Directions:
1. Preheat air fryer to 375°F.
2. Mix coating ingredients in a bowl.
3. Toss zucchini with egg. Dip zucchini into the coating mixture gently pressing to adhere.
4. Lightly spray zucchini with cooking spray.
5. Place in a single layer in the air fryer basket and cook 6 minutes. Turn zucchini over and air fry 6-8 minutes more or until crisp and zucchini is tender.

Notes
For batches, undercook zucchini by 2 minutes. Once all batches are cooked, place them all in the air fryer together for 3 minutes to heat through. Reheat in the air fryer at 375°F for 3-5 minutes or until heated through.

Air Fryer Sweet Potato Cubes
Servings: 3
Cooking Time: 10 Minutes

Ingredients:
- 1 large sweet potato, or two medium ones
- 1 tablespoon olive oil
- 1 teaspoon brown sugar (optional)
- ½ teaspoon salt
- ½ teaspoon dried parsley
- Fresh parsley for garnish (optional)

Directions:
1. Preheat your air fryer to 400F.
2. Peel and slice the sweet potato into ½ inch cubes, you should have 2-2 ½ cups sweet potato cubes.
3. Place sweet potato cubes into a large mixing bowl, drizzle with oil and sprinkle seasonings, then toss to combine.
4. Add the seasoned sweet potato to the air fryer, then cook for 8-10 minutes, shaking the basket halfway through.
5. Sprinkle parsley and serve warm.

Air Fryer Seasoned French Fries
Servings: 4
Cooking Time: 15 Minutes

Ingredients:
- 4 Russet Potatoes peeled, cut into strips
- 1 tbsp olive oil
- 2 tsp paprika
- 1 tsp kosher salt
- 1 tsp garlic powder
- 1 tsp onion powder
- 1 tsp red pepper flakes
- 1/2 tsp black pepper
- 1/4 tsp cayenne pepper

Directions:
1. Peel, and rinse the potatoes.
2. Using a mandolin slicer or sharp knife, cut the potatoes into strips about ¼ inch in thickness.
3. In a medium bowl, soak the strips of potato in cold water for about 30 minutes, then drain them, and pat them dry with a paper towel.
4. Pour in the olive oil and seasonings, tossing the fries to coat them.
5. Place the fries in the air fryer basket, in a single layer, and cook at 400 degrees F for 15-20 minutes, until they are crispy. Shake the basket halfway through cooking.

VEGETABLE & & VEGETARIAN RECIPES

Quick & Easy Air Fryer Asparagus
Servings: 4
Cooking Time: 7-9 Minutes

Ingredients:
- 1 pound medium to thick asparagus
- 1 teaspoon olive oil
- 1/4 teaspoon kosher salt
- 1/4 teaspoon freshly ground black pepper

Directions:
1. Heat an air fryer to 400°F or 425°F (choose the higher temperature if available). Meanwhile, trim the woody ends from 1 pound asparagus. Transfer to a medium bowl, add 1 teaspoon olive oil and 1/4 teaspoon kosher salt, and toss to coat.
2. Add the asparagus to the air fryer and spread into a single layer. Air fry until the asparagus is tender and slightly crispy on the ends, stopping to shake the basket (or rotate the pans in larger air fryers) about halfway through, 8 to 10 minutes total. Transfer to a serving platter and sprinkle 1/4 teaspoon black pepper evenly over the top.

Storage: Refrigerate leftovers in an airtight container for up to 4 days.

Air Fryer Tofu
Servings: 4
Cooking Time: 10 Minutes

Ingredients:
- 15 oz tofu extra firm
- 1/2 tablespoon olive oil
- 1/2 tablespoon sesame oil
- 2 tablespoons soy sauce
- 1/2 teaspoon garlic powder
- 1/2 teaspoon ground ginger
- 1/4 teaspoon salt

Directions:
1. Preheat the air fryer to 190C/375F.
2. Cube the tofu into bite sizes pieces. Place the tofu on a dishtowel or paper towel to soak up excess moisture.
3. In a large bowl, combine the olive oil, sesame oil, soy sauce, garlic powder, and salt. Add the tofu and mix well, until all the tofu is coated.
4. Generously grease the air fryer basket and add a single layer of tofu to it. Air fry for 10-12 minutes, shaking the basket several times throughout.
5. Once the tofu is golden brown, remove it from the basket and repeat the process until all the tofu is cooked up.

Notes
TO STORE: Store leftover crispy tofu in an airtight container in the fridge for up to 4 days.
TO REHEAT: To reheat air-fried tofu, preheat the air fryer to 375F degrees. Add tofu to the air fryer basket and cook for a few minutes until heated through.
TO FREEZE: You can also freeze air-fried tofu if you have made a big batch. Flash-freeze tofu and transfer it into an airtight bag or container. Keep cooked tofu in the freezer for up to 3 months.

Air Fryer Cauliflower Recipe
Servings: 4
Cooking Time: 7 Minutes

Ingredients:
- 1 head Cauliflower (cut into florets)
- 3 tbsp Olive oil
- 2 tsp Lemon juice
- 3/4 tsp Smoked paprika
- 1/2 tsp Garlic powder
- 1/2 tsp Sea salt
- 1/4 tsp Black pepper

Directions:
1. Preheat the air fryer to 380 degrees F (193 degrees C).
2. Place the cauliflower florets in a large bowl. Drizzle with olive oil and lemon juice. Season with smoked paprika, garlic powder, sea salt, and black pepper. Toss to coat.

3. Add cauliflower to the air fryer basket in a single layer (cook in batches if needed – don't crowd the basket). Cook cauliflower in the air fryer for 7-10 minutes (depending on the size of your florets), shaking the basket halfway through, until browned on the edges.

Greek Style Potatoes
Servings: 4
Ingredients:
- 450g red potatoes, cut in quarters
- 2 tbsp olive oil
- 1 tbsp salt
- 2 tsp dried oregano
- 2 tsp black pepper
- 1 tsp paprika
- 60g red onion, diced
- 120g crumbled feta cheese
- 1 tomato, diced
- 30g sliced black olives
- 2 tbsp lemon juice
- For serving fresh dill

Directions:
1. Insert crisper plate in pan and pan in unit. Preheat unit by selecting AIR FRY, setting temperature to 200°C and setting time to 3 minutes. Select START/STOP to begin.
2. In a large bowl, toss the potatoes with olive oil, salt, oregano, pepper and paprika
3. Place potatoes in the pan; reinsert pan
4. Select AIR FRY, set temperature to 200°C and set time to 18 minutes. Select START/STOP to begin. Shake pan halfway through cooking
5. After 13 minutes, remove pan and add red onion. Shake to incorporate. Reinsert pan to resume cooking
6. When cooking is complete, transfer potatoes to a bowl. Add feta, tomato, olives and lemon juice and toss to combine. Top with fresh dill and serve

Air Fryer Stuffed Portobello Mushrooms
Servings: 4
Cooking Time: 15 Minutes
Ingredients:
- 1 pound Italian sausage or ground beef
- ¼ onion diced
- 2 garlic cloves minced
- 1 green pepper diced
- 2 cups tomato sauce
- 1 tablespoon olive oil
- 4 portobello mushroom caps
- ⅓ cup mozzarella shredded
- 1 tablespoon parmesan cheese shredded

Directions:
1. In a large saucepan cook the sausage, garlic, onion, and pepper until tender. Add tomato sauce and let simmer for 10 minutes or until thick.
2. Preheat the air fryer to 350°F.
3. Scoop out the gills of the mushrooms and wash with cold water. Dry thoroughly and drizzle with olive oil.
4. Place mushrooms in the air fryer basket and cook cap side up for 5 minutes.
5. Once done flip mushrooms over and evenly fill with the sausage filling.
6. Top with mozzarella and parmesan cheese, cook for 8-10 minutes or until mushroom is cooked and cheese is melted.

Notes

Mushrooms get soggy so clean them with a spritz of water, and dry with a paper towel, or brush with a damp paper towel.

Gills and stems can be used in the sauce for extra flavor.

Store leftovers in an airtight container in the refrigerator for up to 3 days. Set the air fryer at 400°F and reheat for 4 minutes.

Air Fryer Roasted Baby Potatoes

Servings: 4
Cooking Time: 15 Minutes

Ingredients:
- 650g baby potatoes, washed, dried and cut into halves
- 3 tbs fresh rosemary, chopped
- 1/2 tsp paprika
- 1 tsp salt
- 1/4 tsp pepper
- 1 tbs garlic powder
- 2 tbs olive oil

Directions:
1. Preheat the air fryer to 200°C.
2. Place the baby potatoes in a medium sized bowl. Sprinkle with rosemary, paprika, salt, pepper, garlic powder, and olive oil. Spread the baby potatoes evenly inside the air fryer basket. Do not overcrowd.
3. Bake in the air fryer for 15 minutes, tossing halfway through the cooking process

Mexican Street Corn

Servings: 4
Cooking Time: 12 Minutes

Ingredients:
- 4 ears corn, husks and silks removed
- 1 cup Mexican crema
- 2 limes, zested and juiced
- ½ cup cotija cheese, finely crumbled
- ⅓ cup cilantro, finely chopped
- 2 tablespoons chile de arbol powder or other chili powder
- Items Needed:
- Empty squeeze bottle with lid
- Funnel (optional)

Directions:
1. Place the cooking pot into the base of the Smart Indoor Grill, followed by the grill grate.
2. Select the Air Grill function on max heat, adjust time to 12 minutes, press Shake, then press Start/Pause to preheat.
3. Place the corn onto the preheated grill grate, then close the lid.
4. Flip the corn halfway through cooking. The Shake Reminder will let you know when.
5. Place the crema and lime juice in a medium bowl and stir until well combined, then transfer into the squeeze bottle. Place the cap onto the squeeze bottle and then set aside until ready to use.

Note: Using a funnel may help transferring the crema to the squeeze bottle. Remove the corn when done and place onto a platter.

Use the squeeze bottle to apply the crema to the top of the corn, then sprinkle the lime zest, cotija cheese, cilantro, and chile powder over the top and serve.

Air Fryer Squash Soup

Servings: 4

Ingredients:
- 2 1/2 lb. butternut squash, peeled, cut into 1-inch pieces
- 2 medium carrots, cut into 1-inch pieces
- 1 large onion, cut into 1/2-inch-thick wedges
- 4 cloves garlic, 2 whole and 2 thinly sliced, divided
- 1 Fresno chile, seeded
- 4 sprigs fresh thyme
- 4 tbsp. olive oil, divided
- Kosher salt
- 2 tbsp. pepitas
- 1/4 tsp. smoked paprika
- Sour cream and crusty bread, for serving

Directions:
1. In large bowl, toss squash, carrots, onion, whole garlic cloves, chile, thyme, 2 tablespoons oil and 3/4 teaspoon salt. Transfer to air-fryer basket and air-fry at 400°F, shaking basket occasionally, until vegetables are tender, 30 minutes. Discard thyme sprigs.
2. Meanwhile, in small skillet on medium, cook sliced garlic in remaining 2 tablespoons oil, stirring, until garlic begins to lightly brown around the edges, 2 minutes. Add pepitas and paprika and a

pinch of salt and cook 1 minute; transfer to a bowl.
3. Transfer all but 1/2 cup squash to blender, add 1 cup water and puree, gradually adding 3 more cups water, pureeing until smooth. Reheat if necessary and serve topped with sour cream and spiced pepitas and with crusty bread if desired. Serve topped with remaining squash.
4. GH Test Kitchen Tip: Freeze leftover soup (without the cream and seeds) in an airtight container for up to 3 months. Thaw overnight in the refrigerator, then warm and top as desired.

Air Fryer Ham And Potato Casserole
Servings: 6
Cooking Time: 25 Minutes

Ingredients:
- 1 can condensed cream of mushroom soup 10.5 ounces
- 1/2 cup milk
- 1/4 teaspoon salt
- 1/4 teaspoon pepper
- 1 pound small red potatoes cut in half
- 1/2 cup onion diced
- 2 cups cooked ham diced

Directions:
1. In a medium bowl, combine the cream of mushroom soup, milk, salt and pepper.
2. Stir together until it's a creamy sauce, and then add in the cut potatoes, diced ham and onion, and one cup of cheese.
3. Once the ingredients are well combined, transfer them to a baking dish that will fit in your air fryer.
4. Air fry at 400° Fahrenheit for 20-25 minutes, until potatoes are soft. Stir the casserole at least two or three times during the cooking process.
5. Once the potatoes are soft, sprinkle shredded cheddar or swiss cheese onto the casserole, and then return to the air fryer and continue cooking for a couple of minutes, until the cheese melts.

6. Optional Toppings:
7. Sprinkle with shredded cheese, cooked stuffing, or dried onions.

NOTES
Because air fryers may have different wattages, cooking time may vary by a few minutes.

Hot Cauliflower Wings
Servings: 4

Ingredients:
- For the wings
- 1/2 head of cauliflower, cut into florets
- 1 cup of flour, you can use gluten free flour
- 1 1/2 cup of coconut milk
- 1/2 tsp smoked paprika powder
- 1/3 tsp harrisa powder
- salt and black pepper
- 1/2 tsp garlic powder
- For the sauce
- 1 cup of bbq sauce
- 2 tbsp sweet and sour sauce
- 2 tbsp tomato puree
- 2 tbsp lemon juice
- 2 tbsp honey
- 1 tbsp sriracha sauce (optional)

Directions:
1. Start by chopping cauliflower to smaller florets.
2. Prepare the batter by placing in the bowl; coconut milk, spices, salt & pepper and flour. Mix until everything is well incorporated.
3. Preheat your ninja electric grill on air frying mode to 200C.
4. Coat each cauliflower floret in the batter. Shake off the excess of the batter.
5. Place them in the air fryer cooking basket, don't place them to close together, as they will stick.
6. Once that's done, set the time to 10 min. Shake the florets half way the time, make sure they crisp evenly on both sides.
7. Make the sauce by placing all ingredients in the small pot. Cook for 5-7 min on a

medium heat steering. The sauce should thicken a bit.
8. Coat each baked cauliflower florets in the sauce.
9. Serve hot.

Moroccan Spiced Carrots

Servings: 4
Cooking Time: 12 Minutes

Ingredients:
- 450g carrots
- 1 1/2 tbs olive oil
- 1/2 tsp cumin
- 1/2 tsp ground coriander
- 1/4 tsp cinnamon
- 1/4 tsp sweet paprika
- 1/4 tsp ground ginger

Directions:
1. Whisk the spice mix together in a small bowl. Add the oil to a large bowl and toss the carrots to coat. Sprinkle over the spices and mix well.
2. Heat the air fryer to 180°C and cook the carrots for 10-12 minutes until crisp, turning halfway through.

Oven Baked Buffalo Cauliflower

Servings: 8
Cooking Time: 30 Minutes

Ingredients:
- 1 head of cauliflower washed and dried
- 1 cup milk
- 1 cup flour
- 1 tablespoon olive oil
- 1 teaspoon garlic powder
- pepper to taste
- ⅔ cup Panko bread crumbs
- ⅔ cup buffalo sauce (see note below)

Directions:
1. Preheat oven to 450°F.
2. Cut cauliflower into bite-sized pieces and discard the core.
3. Combine milk, flour, oil, garlic powder, and pepper in a large bowl. Place batter and cauliflower in a large zippered bag and gently toss until cauliflower is coated.
4. Pour cauliflower into a large strainer, letting any excess batter drip off. You want just a light coating of batter. Sprinkle with Panko breadcrumbs and gently toss.
5. Place on a foil-lined pan and bake for 15 minutes. Remove from the oven and gently toss with buffalo sauce. You want the cauliflower coated but not soaked.
6. Place cauliflower back on the pan and bake for an additional 5-10 minutes or until cauliflower is tender-crisp.
7. Serve with ranch or blue cheese dressing.

Notes
Note: You can purchase store-bought buffalo sauce or mix ⅓ cup melted butter with ⅔ cup hot sauce (such as Frank's Red Hot). Whisk until combined.
Ensure the cauliflower is very dry after washing. You can use a salad spinner or shake it dry. I try to wash it the day before if I can.
Toss the cauliflower in the wet batter and let most of the excess drip off, you want just a light coating.
Gently add some of the buffalo sauce to the cauliflower, you don't want them saturated with sauce or they will get soggy.
If some of your friends/family don't like spice, leave a few aside when adding buffalo sauce and season with salt and black pepper instead. Serve them with your favorite dips.

Crispy Air Fryer Lemon Broccoli

Servings: 4
Cooking Time: 8 Minutes

Ingredients:
- 300g broccoli, chopped into florets
- 1 1/2 tbs olive oil
- 1 tsp garlic powder
- 1 lemon, 1 tsp zest
- 1/4 tsp chilli flakes
- 1 pinch black pepper (to taste)

Directions:

1. Place the broccoli florets in a large bowl, add the oil, garlic powder, lemon zest, chilli flakes and black pepper and toss well to coat.
2. Heat the air fryer to 180°C and cook the broccoli for 8 minutes, shaking halfway through.

Air Fryer Fried Pickles

Servings: 4
Cooking Time: 10 Minutes

Ingredients:
- 2 cups dill pickle slices
- 1/2 cup flour
- 1 large egg
- 1 Tablespoon water
- 1/2 cup bread crumbs
- 1/4 cup grated Parmesan
- 1 Tablespoon Italian seasoning

Directions:
1. Lay the pickles on a paper towel and pat dry. In the first small bowl add the flour. In the second small bowl add the egg and whisk with the water. In the last bowl add the bread crumbs, parmesan, and italian seasoning.
2. Dip each pickle in the flour, then the egg and lastly in the bread crumb mixture.
3. Lay the pickles in a single layer in the air fryer basket. Cook at 400 degrees for 8-10 minutes. Serve with your favorite dipping sauce.

Air Fryer Cauliflower 'wings'

Servings: 4
Cooking Time: 10-30 Minutes

Ingredients:
- 1 small–medium cauliflower, cut the cauliflower into florets, approx. 4–6cm/1½–2½in, save the stalk and leaves for another recipe
- 125g/4½oz plain flour
- 1 tsp baking powder
- 1 tsp paprika
- cooking oil spray
- 2–3 tbsp buffalo hot sauce (check that it's vegan)
- salt and freshly ground black pepper
- For the dip
- 175g/6oz unsweetened oat-based yoghurt
- 1 small garlic clove, crushed or finely grated
- 1 lemon, zest only, plus juice of ½ lemon
- 3 tbsp finely chopped fresh herbs, such as coriander, chives, dill, mint – or a mix

Directions:
1. Preheat the air fryer to 200C.
2. Put the flour, baking powder and paprika in a bowl with some salt and pepper. Whisk in 150ml/¼ pint cold water to make a thick batter. Dip the cauliflower florets in to coat them and set aside on a plate.
3. Spray the air fryer basket with oil, then add the florets in a single layer (they can be touching: you can break them apart after cooking). Spray the tops with more oil and air-fry for 10 minutes, or until golden brown and crispy but cooked through. (You may need to cook in two batches.)
4. Meanwhile, make the dip. Mix the yoghurt, garlic, lemon zest and juice together in a bowl, then stir in the chopped herbs and season to taste.
5. If you cooked the cauliflower in batches, put all the florets back into the air fryer and heat for 1 minute.
6. Put 2 tablespoons of the hot sauce into a big bowl. Tip in the hot cauliflower florets and mix to coat all of the pieces. Serve immediately, drizzled with the third tablespoon of hot sauce if you dare, and the cooling dip alongside.

NOTES

This recipe was made in an air fryer without a paddle attachment. The batter needs to set on the cauliflower until it is crisp before it will come away from the air fryer basket.

No air fryer? Preheat the oven to 200C/180C Fan/Gas 6. Line a baking sheet with baking paper, spray with cooking oil and bake the battered cauliflower florets for 20 minutes, until crispy.

Air Fryer Squash

Servings: 4
Cooking Time: 7 Minutes

Ingredients:
- 1 medium summer squash or zucchini
- ½ teaspoon Italian seasoning
- 1 tablespoon olive oil
- salt & pepper to taste

Directions:
1. Slice squash or zucchini into ½" slices.
2. Toss with olive oil and seasonings.
3. Preheat air fryer to 400°F.
4. Add squash and cook 6-7 minutes or until tender crisp. Cook for 2 minutes longer if you prefer a softer squash.

Air Fryer Asparagus

Servings: 4
Cooking Time: 7 Minutes

Ingredients:
- 1 pound asparagus
- 1 tablespoon olive oil
- salt and pepper to taste

Directions:
1. Preheat the air fryer to 400°F.
2. Wash and dry the asparagus trimming the ends*.
3. Toss the asparagus with the oil and seasonings.
4. Place in the air fryer basket and cook for 7-10 minutes or until tender.

Notes
To trim the ends: Hold the stalk and bend it until the thick end snaps off (about 1 to 2 inches from the end). Line up the remaining stalks and cut them to the same length.

Air Fryer Vegetables

Servings: 4
Cooking Time: 9 Minutes

Ingredients:
- 1 small zucchini sliced
- 2 bell peppers diced
- 1 ½ tablespoon olive oil
- 1 teaspoon Italian seasoning
- 1 garlic clove minced
- salt and pepper to taste

Directions:
1. Preheat air fryer to 380°F.
2. In a large bowl mix vegetables, garlic, seasonings, and oil together until evenly coated.
3. Add to the air fryer basket and cook for 7-9 minutes or until tender-crisp.

Notes
Cut veggies in uniformly and avoid overfilling the air fryer so the veggies evenly cook.

Air Fryer Crispy Broccoli With Cheese

Servings: 4
Cooking Time: 15 Minutes

Ingredients:
- 1 pound (454 g) broccoli, cut into bite-sized pieces
- 2 Tablespoons (30 ml) olive oil, approximately
- 1/2 teaspoon (2.5 ml) garlic powder
- salt, to taste
- black pepper, to taste
- 4 oz. (113 g) shredded cheddar cheese, or cheese of preference

Directions:
1. Cut the fresh broccoli into even bite sized pieces.
2. Add the broccoli to a large bowl. Coat the broccoli with oil. Season broccoli with garlic powder, salt and pepper.
3. Add the raw broccoli to the air fryer basket or rack. Air Fry 380°F/193°C for 10 minutes then flip, turn or shake halfway through cooking (about 5 minutes) to ensure that the broccoli cooks evenly.
4. Cooking times will vary depending on the size of your broccoli and size/power of your air fryer.

5. If you like your broccoli more crispy, add additional 1-2 minutes of air frying time.
6. Add cheese on top of broccoli and cook for about 1 minute, or until cheese is melted.
7. After cheese has melted, transfer to a bowl or you can eat it straight out of the air fryer!

Air Fryer Baby Potatoes

Servings: 4
Cooking Time: 20 Minutes

Ingredients:
- 1 pound baby potatoes
- 1 tablespoon olive oil
- 1 clove garlic minced
- ¼ teaspoon rosemary chopped
- ¼ teaspoon salt and pepper each

Directions:
1. Preheat the air fryer to 400°F.
2. Combine the potatoes, oil, garlic, and seasonings and mix until evenly coated.
3. Place in the air fryer and cook for 18-20 minutes, shaking the basket halfway through.
4. Cook until tender and browned.

Notes
Refrigerate leftovers in an airtight container for up to 3 days.
Freeze leftovers in a zippered bag for up to 6 weeks.

Baked Eggplant Sticks

Servings: 4
Cooking Time: 15 Minutes

Ingredients:
- 10 oz eggplant (from 1 small or 1/2 large)
- 1 tsp olive oil
- 1/2 tsp kosher salt and fresh cracked pepper
- 1/2 cup Italian seasoned breadcrumbs ((substitute with gluten bread crumbs if GF))
- 2 tbsp Parmesan cheese
- 1 large egg white
- oil spray
- 1 cup quick marinara sauce for dipping (optional, extra)

Directions:
1. Oven **Directions:**
2. Preheat the oven to 450°F. Line two baking sheets with parchment paper and lightly spray with oil.
3. Place eggplant strips in a bowl and season with olive oil, salt and pepper. Set aside.
4. Combine breadcrumbs and parmesan cheese in a bowl, and egg whites in another.
5. Dip a few strips of eggplant at a time into the egg whites, then into the breadcrumbs. Using a fork, remove eggplant from crumbs and place on the baking sheets. Spray with more oil and bake 10 minutes in the middle rack.
6. Turn over and bake an additional 5 minutes, or until golden. Serve hot.

Air Fryer Directions:
Cook in batches, putting the sticks in the basket in an even layer, careful not to overcrowd it. Spritz with olive oil spray. Air Fry at 350F for 10 minutes, turning halfway.

Air Fryer Baked Potato

Servings: 1
Cooking Time: 30 Minutes-1 Hour

Ingredients:
- 1 baking potato (see recipe tips and weigh before cooking), scrubbed and dried
- light rapeseed, vegetable or sunflower oil
- salt and freshly ground black pepper
- For the cheddar and jalapeño topping
- small handful grated cheddar
- 1 ripe tomato, diced
- few green jalapeño pepper slices from a jar
- For the smashed avocado topping
- 1 small, ripe avocado (or a few frozen avocado slices)
- ½ lime or lemon, juice only
- handful mixed seeds, dukkah, za'atar or chilli flakes
- For the curried beans topping

- 227g tin baked beans
- ½ tsp curry powder
- natural yoghurt and lime pickle (optional), to serve

Directions:
1. Rub the potato all over with a little oil. If you like, rub a little salt over the skin – this will help give a crispier finish.
2. Put the potato in the air fryer and turn to 200C (you don't want to preheat, to avoid burning the skin before the inside is cooked.) Air-fry for 20 minutes, then turn the potato over. A small potato will take another 20 minutes or so, a large one another 25–30 minutes.
3. Check the middle is soft by poking a table knife into the centre – it should slide in easily. If it's not quite done, continue to cook for a minute at a time.
4. For the cheddar and jalapeño topping, mix the cheese, tomato and jalapeño slices, split the potato and spoon the cheese mixture on top.
5. For the smashed avocado topping, mash the avocado with the lime or lemon juice, salt and pepper. Split the potato, spoon in the avocado mixture and scatter with the seeds or your choice of seasoning.
6. For the curried beans topping, heat the beans with the curry powder until hot but not boiling. Split the potato and pile on the beans. Top with dollops of yoghurt and lime pickle, if using.

NOTES

Small potatoes, around 225g/8oz each, will be ready in 40 minutes. Large potatoes, around 350g/12oz each, will take 45–50 minutes to get soft inside.

You can speed up the cooking by microwaving your jacket potatoes first. Microwave on high power for four minutes, turn the potato over, and microwave for another four minutes. (If you are cooking two potatoes, you may need to microwave them for an extra 2 minutes.) Then cook in the air-fryer for 10 minutes to crisp up. Look for potatoes labelled as bakers, or a floury variety, such as King Edward, Maris Piper, Vivaldi or Estima.

Air Fryer Potatoes

Servings: 2
Cooking Time: 15 Minutes

Ingredients:
- 3 yukon gold potatoes quartered
- 1 teaspoon olive oil
- 1/8 teaspoon paprika
- 1/8 teaspoon garlic powder
- Salt and pepper to taste
- Cooking spray

Directions:
1. Preheat the air fryer 380°F.
2. Toss the potatoes in a bowl with the olive oil, paprika and garlic powder. Season with salt and pepper, and toss to coat.
3. Place the potato wedges in the basket of the air fryer, without over crowding the pan. Cook for 8 minutes, then use tongs to flip and cook for an additional 5-7 minutes.
4. Remove and enjoy immediately with ketchup, if desired

Notes

Storage: Store any leftovers in an airtight container. They will last about 3-4 days in the fridge. To reheat, just place in the airfryer at 360°F for 1-2 minutes or in a toaster oven. You can also reheat in the microwave but the potatoes won't retain their crispy texture that way.

Substitutes: For best results, follow the recipe as is. However you can switch out the spices if you'd like and use other types of potatoes.

Equipment: I just bought the NuWave air fryer a couple months ago and I used this to make this recipe and many more recipes. It's easy to use with guides on the appliance, easy to clean up and I've been very happy with the results!

SALADS & SIDE DISHES RECIPES

Cardamom Roasted Beetroot Salad With Harissa Tahini Sauce

Servings: 4

Ingredients:
- For the roasted beets
- 500g beetroot (peeled, chopped into 2cm pieces)
- 1 x 400g organic chickpeas (drained, rinsed, patted dry)
- 1 1/2 tbsp olive oil
- 1 tbsp agave nectar
- 2 tsp ground cumin
- 16 Seeds from green cardamom pods (ground in pestle and mortar)
- 1 1/4 tsp sea salt
- 1/2 tsp garlic powder
- 1/4 tsp ground black pepper
- 1 Zest of lemon
- For the sauce
- 80g light tahini
- 190ml lukewarm water
- 1 tbsp rose harissa
- 2 tsp agave nectar
- 1 clove garlic (peeled)
- 1 tsp red wine vinegar
- 1/4 tsp ground cumin
- 1/4 - 1/2 tsp sea salt
- 1/2 - 1 Juice of whole lemon
- For the salad
- 100g pomegranate seeds (roughly 1/2 pomegranate)
- 60g rocket
- 30g walnuts (roughly chopped)
- 20g fresh parsley (roughly chopped)
- 1/2 tsp za'atar
- COOKING MODE
- When entering cooking mode - We will enable your screen to stay 'always on' to avoid any unnecessary interruptions whilst you cook!

Directions:
1. Toss together all of the ingredients for the roasted beets in a large bowl until everything is fully coated.
2. Place the crisper tray into the zone 1 drawer then add the vegetables and insert the drawer back into the unit. Select ROAST, set the temperature to 180°C and the temperature to 25 minutes. Select START/STOP to begin cooking. Shake the drawer every 10 minutes until the cooking time is complete. Remove the drawer and set to one side.
3. Place the ingredients for the sauce into a bullet style blender and blend until smooth. Start with the juice of half a lemon and add more if you feel it needs it. Again if you'd prefer a thinner sauce blend in more water.
4. Toss together the roasted beetroot mixture in a large salad bowl with the remaining salad ingredients then serve immediately with plenty of the sauce drizzled over.

Air Fryer Roasted Butternut Squash Salad

Servings: 4
Cooking Time: 15 Minutes

Ingredients:
- 1 small butternut squash, peeled, seeded, cut into 1-inch pieces
- 4 tablespoons olive oil
- 1 teaspoon 's House Seasoning
- 1/4 teaspoon cayenne pepper
- 2 tablespoons fresh lemon juice
- 1 small shallot, minced
- 1/4 teaspoon salt
- 6 ounces arugula
- 1 small Granny Smith apple, cored and thinly sliced
- 1/2 cup toasted sliced almonds
- 1/2 cup grated Parmesan cheese

Directions:
1. In a large bowl, combine squash, 2 tablespoons of the olive oil, House

Seasoning, and cayenne pepper; toss to coat well.
2. Place squash in air fryer basket, set air fryer temperature to 400 degrees, and cook for 15 minutes, shaking occasionally. Let cool.
3. In a large bowl, whisk together lemon juice, shallot, salt, and remaining olive oil. Add arugula and toss to coat. Divide arugula between 4 salad plates and top with squash and apple slices. Sprinkle with sliced almonds and Parmesan cheese. Serve chilled.

Air Fryer Pigs In A Blanket

Servings: 10
Cooking Time: 8 Minutes

Ingredients:
- 1 can crescent rolls
- 24 cocktail sausages

Directions:
1. Preheat the air fryer to 350 degrees Fahrenheit. Prepare the air fryer basket with nonstick cooking spray, or once the air fryer has been preheated, add parchment paper.
2. Take a pizza cutter and slice each crescent dough sheet into thirds.
3. Take the cut crescent dough and wrap the dough around the sausage.
4. Place the crescent dogs into the prepared air fryer basket in a single layer and make sure to allow an inch or two between each crescent sausage. You may need to cook in batches if needed.
5. Air fry on 350 degrees Fahrenheit for 3-4 minutes, flip, and then air fry for an additional 3-4 minutes, or until the crescents are golden brown.
6. Carefully remove from the air fryer basket and serve with your favorite dipping sauces.

NOTES
This recipe was made using the Cosori 5.8 qt air fryer. If you are using a different air fryer, your cook time may need to be adjusted up or down depending on the wattage and power of the heating element.

WHAT DIPPING SAUCES CAN I USE FOR PIGS IN A BLANKET?
I love to use ketchup and mustard, but you can also use bbq sauce, cheese sauce, honey mustard sauce, ranch dressing, and more.
CAN I COOK FROZEN PIGS IN A BLANKET IN THE AIR FRYER?
Absolutely! If you are cooking these pigs in a blanket from frozen, you will want to add a minute or two to the cooking time to ensure they are cooked completely.

Air Fryer Asparagus Salad With Feta Vinaigrette

Servings: 4

Ingredients:
- 1 lb. asparagus
- 2 tbsp. olive oil, divided
- Kosher salt and pepper
- 1 tbsp. rice vinegar
- 1 small shallot, finely chopped
- 1/4 c. fresh mint, finely chopped
- 2 oz. feta, crumbled
- 2 tbsp. fresh dill, roughly chopped

Directions:
1. Heat oven to 425°F. On a small rimmed baking sheet, toss asparagus with 1 tablespoon oil and ¼ teaspoon each salt and pepper. Roast until just tender, 8 to 12 minutes; transfer to platter.
2. Meanwhile, in small bowl, combine vinegar, shallot and ¼ teaspoon each salt and pepper. Let sit, tossing occasionally, until asparagus is done.
3. Stir remaining tablespoon oil into shallot mixture, then gently toss with mint and feta. Spoon over asparagus and sprinkle with dill.

AIR FRYING INSTRUCTIONS:
Heat air fryer to 400°F. Toss asparagus with 1 tablespoon olive oil and 1/4 teaspoon each salt and pepper. Air-fry, shaking basket halfway through, until tender, 10 minutes. Proceed with steps 2-3.

Crispy Parmesan Potato Wedges

Servings: 2

Ingredients:
- 2 small russet potatoes
- 2 tablespoons (28 grams) Parmesan cheese, grated
- ¾ teaspoon (4 grams) salt
- ¼ teaspoon (2 grams) garlic powder
- ¼ teaspoon (2 grams) paprika
- ¼ teaspoon (2 grams) dried oregano
- 1 tablespoon (15 milliliters) neutral-flavored oil

Directions:
1. Cut each potato lengthwise into 8 wedges and place them in a large bowl.
2. Add the remaining ingredients and toss to coat.
3. Place the crisper plate into the Smart Air Fryer basket, then place the potatoes onto the crisper plate.
4. Select the Fries function, adjust time to 22 minutes, and press Start/Pause.
5. Remove the potato wedges when done and serve.

Air Fryer Roasted Garlic

Servings: 1/2
Cooking Time: 10 Minutes

Ingredients:
- 3 full bulbs garlic
- 1-2 tablespoons olive oil
- 1 teaspoon salt

Directions:
1. Preheat air fryer to 400 F
2. Carefully slice the tops off the garlic bulbs; the cloves inside should be exposed.
3. Drizzle the olive oil over top of each garlic bulb, making sure all the cloves get covered.
4. Sprinkle salt on each bulb and tightly wrap each in tin foil.
5. Place garlic into your air fryer and cook for 18-20 minutes, or until garlic is tender.
6. Allow to cool until you can handle and remove the bulbs from the papery skin.

Air Fryer Garlic Knots

Servings: 6
Cooking Time: 8 Minutes

Ingredients:
- 1 can store-bought pizza dough 13.8 ounces or two cans of thin crust pizza 8 ounces each
- 4 tablespoons unsalted butter melted
- 1/4 cup parmesan cheese grated
- 2 cloves garlic minced
- 1 tablespoon dried parsley flakes
- 1 teaspoon Italian Seasoning

Directions:
1. Open the can of premade pizza dough and on a lightly floured surface, roll it out into a rectangle.
2. With a pizza cutter or kitchen knife cut the dough into twelve 1-inch strips, and then fold each strip in half. Tie each piece into dough knots, making 12 knots.
3. Place the dough balls into the air fryer basket in a single layer, lined with parchment paper, a silicone baking mat or lightly sprayed with olive oil spray.
4. Air fry at 350 degrees F for 8-10 minutes, until they are golden brown.
5. While knots are in a small mixing bowl, stir together the melted butter, parmesan cheese, garlic, parsley flakes, and Italian seasoning.
6. When knots are golden brown, use a pastry brush and generously brush garlic butter on each piece with butter and seasonings and top with grated parmesan cheese.

NOTES

Kitchen Tips: Make these in batches without overcrowding the basket. Use a food scale to ensure they are all the same size, so they cook evenly. To get a deeper brown color cook for 1 additional minute.

If using regular crust dough, knots will be just a tad bit thicker and may need 1-2 additional minutes of air frying time.

For smaller bites, just cut the dough in half, and you will have 24 garlic knots.

Optional Favorite Dipping Sauce: Our favorite sauce for dipping is marinara. But you can use other sauces, like homemade marinara sauce, alfredo sauce, pesto sauce, pizza sauce or Greek yogurt with roasted garlic.

Artichoke Wings With Vegan Ranch Dip

Servings: 6

Ingredients:
- Artichoke Wings
- One 16-ounce jar marinated artichoke hearts
- 1½ cups all-purpose flour
- 1 teaspoon garlic powder
- 1 teaspoon onion powder
- 1 teaspoon paprika
- 1 teaspoon kosher salt
- One 12-ounce bottle beer (Lager or Weisse-style for best results)
- 2 cups panko breadcrumbs
- Vegan Ranch Dip
- 1 cup vegan mayonnaise
- ¼ cup non-dairy milk (i.e., coconut, oat, or any nut milk)
- 2 tablespoons fresh dill, finely chopped
- 1 teaspoon fresh Italian parsley leaves, finely chopped
- 1 teaspoon vegan Worcestershire sauce (optional)
- 1 teaspoon apple cider vinegar
- 1 teaspoon lemon juice
- 1 clove garlic, grated
- 1 teaspoon onion powder
- 1 teaspoon black pepper
- Kosher salt, to taste
- Oil spray

Directions:
1. Select the Preheat function on the Air Fryer then press Start/Pause.
2. Drain the artichoke hearts and pat dry with paper towels.
3. Whisk together the flour, garlic powder, onion powder, paprika, and salt in a large bowl until evenly distributed.
4. Pour in the beer and whisk well until no lumps remain. The mixture should resemble pancake batter.
5. Place the panko breadcrumbs in a separate medium bowl.
6. Line the preheated air fryer baskets with parchment paper.
7. Dredge the artichoke hearts in the beer batter, then roll in the panko breadcrumbs.
8. Shake off any excess breadcrumbs, then place the dredged artichoke hearts into the lined air fryer baskets.
9. Spray the wings lightly with oil and insert into the preheated air fryer.
10. Adjust temperature to 400°F and time to 10 minutes, press Shake, then press Start/Pause.
11. Flip the wings and spray again halfway through cooking. The Shake Reminder will let you know when.
12. Combine all the dressing ingredients in a separate medium bowl and whisk together.
13. Season to taste with kosher salt. Pour into a bowl for dipping.
14. Remove the artichoke wings from the air fryer when done.
15. Serve immediately with the vegan ranch dressing.

Air Fryer Sweet Potato Casserole

Servings: 6
Cooking Time: 10 Minutes

Ingredients:
- 29 ounce sweet potato yams drained
- 3/4 cup pecans
- 1/4 teaspoon salt
- 1 egg
- 1/2 teaspoon vanilla extract
- 1/4 teaspoon ground cinnamon
- 1 1/4 cup granulated white sugar
- 1 Tablespoon heavy cream
- 2 Tablespoons unsalted butter softened

Directions:
1. Preheat the air fryer to 350 degrees Fahrenheit.

2. Place the sweet potatoes into a medium sized mixing bowl. Add the salt, butter, egg, vanilla extract, ground cinnamon, white sugar, and heavy cream. Mix thoroughly for one minute.
3. Place the pecans in a food processor. Chop the pecans until they are small and easy to sprinkle.
4. Take the sweet potato mixture and place in a prepared 7" springform pan. Cover the top with the chopped pecans.
5. Place the springform pan into the air fryer basket. Air fry for 10-12 minutes or until the topping is browned.

NOTES

Can I make a sweet potato casserole in the air fryer with a marshmallow topping?

Yes, you can, but you may want to consider doing it a little differently than the traditional method of topping the casserole with mini marshmallows. Because marshmallows are light and fluffy, they can easily blow around and possibly blow up into the heating element.If you want to have a marshmallow topping, consider using the jarred marshmallow fluff, or push the marshmallows into the casserole so that they don't fly around while air frying.

How do I store leftover sweet potato casserole?

Store leftover sweet potato casserole in an airtight container in the refrigerator for up to 4 days.

How do I reheat leftover air fryer sweet potato casserole?

To reheat leftover casserole, add it to an oven-safe dish and reheat in the air fryer at 350 degrees Fahrenheit for 2-3 minutes, or until the casserole is heated through.

What are additions I can make to sweet potato casserole?

You can change the flavors in sweet potato casserole by adding different ingredients such as diced pineapple. It gives the casserole an even more pronounced flavor and it is delicious!

Air Fryer Diced Potatoes

Servings: 4
Cooking Time: 20 Minutes

Ingredients:
- 1 ½ pounds of small potatoes
- 2 cups cold water
- 1 tablespoon fresh thyme or 1 teaspoon dried thyme
- ½ tablespoon minced garlic
- ½ tablespoon olive oil
- Juice of 1/2 a lemon, about 2 tablespoons of a medium size lemon
- Salt to taste

Directions:
1. Wash your potatoes and dice them into small cubes. The closer they are in size, the more evenly they will cook.
2. Soak the cut potatoes for 10 minutes in cold water. This will help remove some starch and allow them to crisp up more. Once they have soaked, drain them and then pat them dry with a paper towel.
3. Combine potatoes with the thyme, garlic, olive oil and lemon juice.
4. Place diced potatoes in your air fryer basket. Cook at 380 degrees F for 20 to 25 minutes, giving the basket a good shake at the 10 minute mark.

NOTES
OPTIONAL

Sprinkle more fresh thyme to the potatoes before serving or some zest from your lemon, or both!

HOW TO REHEAT DICED POTATOES IN THE AIR FRYER

Preheat the air fryer to 350 degrees F.
Lay the leftover diced potatoes in the air fryer basket in a single layer.
Cook for 3 to 5 minutes until heated through.

BEEF, PORK & LAMB RECIPES

Air Fryer Bacon Wrapped Serranos

Ingredients:
- 12 Serrano peppers
- 12 Slices partially Cooked bacon
- 2 String Mozarella Cheeses

Directions:
1. Partially cook the bacon in the air fryer at 300° for 3 minutes on each side. Place onto paper towel and set aside.
2. Cut the tops off the serrano peppers and carefully slice down one side of the pepper(do not cut all the way through). Fold open the pepper and remove seeds.
3. Peel pieces of the string cheese and stuff the peppers. Wrap the bacon around each pepper tightly then place into air fryer basket.
4. Air fry at 350° for 5 minutes or until desired bacon crispiness.

Air Fryer Breaded Pork Chops

Servings: 4
Cooking Time: 8 Minutes

Ingredients:
- 4-6 pork chops 1.5 pounds
- ¼ cup egg whites, whisked about 2 large egg whites
- ¾ cup Italian breadcrumbs
- ½ tsp Italian seasoning
- ½ tsp ground black pepper
- olive oil spray

Directions:
1. Use shallow bowls to create a dredging station by adding egg whites into one shallow bowl and make breadcrumb mixture with Italian seasoning, and ground black pepper into the other shallow bowl. Set both bowls aside.
2. Pat pork chops dry with paper towels on a cutting board or baking sheet.
3. Dip each pork chop into the egg whites, and then into the breading mixture until each piece is fully coated.
4. Place the breaded pork chops on a baking sheet or clean plate until all pieces have been breaded.
5. Prepare the air fryer basket with air fryer safe cooking spray, then place the pork chops in a single layer to allow room for the air to circulate and even cooking.
6. Very lightly spray the tops of the pork chops with olive oil spray. Air fry at 380 degrees F for 8-10 minutes, flipping and spraying cutlets with cooking spray again halfway through the cooking process for maximum crispiness.
7. Check the internal temperature of the pork with a meat thermometer. Temperature should be 145 degrees F.
8. Remove from the basket when they are cooked through and golden brown. Place them on a wire rack to remain crispy.

NOTES
Variations
Change the seasonings - You can easily add garlic powder, onion powder, or even some cayenne pepper to these pork chops to change the flavor.
Use a different crust - I love using Italian breadcrumbs, but this amazing air fryer recipe would work well with panko breadcrumbs as well.

Air Fryer Cheese Stuffed Meatballs

Servings: 4
Cooking Time: 7 Minutes

Ingredients:
- 1 pound ground beef
- 1 cup Italian Seasoned Breadcrumbs
- 1/2 cup parmesan cheese grated or shredded
- 1 large egg
- 1 teaspoon garlic minced
- 1/2 teaspoon kosher salt

- 1/4 teaspoon ground black pepper
- 4 pieces string cheese cut into inch in pieces

Directions:
1. In a medium mixing bowl, combine beef, breadcrumbs, parmesan cheese, egg, garlic, salt, and pepper. Stir until meatball mixture is well combined.
2. Use a large spoon or cookie scoop to measure them so they are all the same size (about 2-3 tablespoons of meat).
3. Roll each scoopful into about 2-inch sized meatballs (about the size of a golf ball). Place them on a plate or baking sheet until they are all rolled.
4. Cut string cheese into small pieces, about 1 inch in length. Push a cheese cube into the center of each meatball, and then close them back up around the piece of cheese, by reshaping the meatball to seal in the cheese.
5. Spray the air fryer basket with cooking spray and place the meatballs in a single layer to the basket.
6. Air fry at 380 degrees F for 7-10 minutes, until the hamburger meat is done. To make sure it's done, use a meat thermometer to read the internal temperature, minimum temperature should be about 160 degrees F.

NOTES

Optional Favorite Sauce for Dipping: Because meatballs are so versatile, you can eat them with your favorite marinara sauce, pizza sauce, alfredo sauce, pesto sauce or ranch dressing.

Kitchen Tips: This recipe will make a couple of batches of meatballs. Line basket with parchment paper so meatballs won't stick to the basket and makes for an easier clean up.

Substitutions: If you don't have lean ground beef, you can also use ground turkey, ground lamb, ground chicken, ground pork or a lean ground beef. Mini mozzarella balls are also a great stuffer.

Air Fryer Chuck Roast

Servings: 6
Cooking Time: 45 Minutes

Ingredients:
- 2 pounds beef chuck roast
- 1 tablespoon olive oil
- ½ tablespoon Worcestershire sauce
- 1 ½ teaspoons kosher salt
- 1 ½ teaspoons garlic powder
- 1 teaspoon onion powder
- 1 teaspoon dried thyme
- 1 teaspoon dried rosemary
- 1 teaspoon black pepper

Directions:
1. Line the inside of your air fryer with aluminum foil. Preheat the air fryer to 390 degrees F.
2. In a small bowl, whisk together olive oil and Worcestershire sauce. In a second small bowl, combine the salt, garlic powder, onion powder, thyme, rosemary, and pepper.
3. Rub the roast with the olive oil-Worcestershire sauce mixture, then rub the herb mixture over the entire roast. Place the roast in the basket of your air fryer.
4. Air fry for 15 minutes, then carefully flip the roast. Air fry at 320 degrees F for another 45-60 minutes, depending on the size of the roast.
5. Remove, allow to rest for 10 minutes, then slice and serve with your favorite sides.

Air Fryer Gingery Pork Meatballs

Servings: 4

Ingredients:
- FOR NOODLES
- 6 oz. rice noodles
- 1/2 c. Asian-style sesame dressing
- 1 large carrot, shaved with julienne peeler or cut into matchsticks
- 1/2 English cucumber, shaved with julienne peeler or cut into matchsticks
- 1 scallion, thinly sliced

- 1/4 c. cilantro, chopped
- FOR MEATBALLS
- 1 large egg
- 2 tsp. grated lime zest plus 2 Tbsp lime juice
- 1 1/2 tbsp. honey
- 1 tsp. fish sauce
- Kosher salt
- 1/2 c. panko
- 1 cloves garlic, grated
- 2 scallions, finely chopped
- 1 tbsp. grated fresh ginger
- 1 small jalapeño, seeds removed, finely chopped
- 1 lb. ground pork
- 1/4 c. cilantro, chopped

Directions:
1. Prepare noodles: Cook noodles per package directions. Rinse under cold water to cool, drain well and transfer to large bowl. Toss with dressing, carrot, cucumber and scallion; set aside.
2. Prepare meatballs: In large bowl, whisk together egg, lime zest and lime juice, honey, fish sauce and ? teaspoon salt; stir in panko and let sit 1 minute. Stir in garlic, scallions, ginger and jalapeño, then add pork and cilantro and mix to combine.
3. Shape into Tbsp-size balls and air-fry at 400F (in batches, if necessary; balls can touch but should not be stacked), shaking basket occasionally, until browned and cooked through, 8 to 12 minutes. Fold cilantro into noodles and serve with meatballs.

Air Fryer Pork Roast
Servings: 6
Cooking Time: 1 Hour

Ingredients:
- 2 pound boneless pork loin roast
- 1/3 cup brown sugar
- 2 teaspoons kosher salt
- 1 1/2 teaspoons garlic powder
- 1 teaspoon smoked paprika
- 1/2 teaspoon onion powder
- 1/2 teaspoon dried thyme leaves
- 1/2 teaspoon black pepper
- SERVE WITH potatoes, rice, steamed vegetables

Directions:
1. Pat the pork roast dry. Combine the seasonings in a small bowl, then rub the mixture over the pork. Wrap the roast tightly in plastic wrap and refrigerate for 4-24 hours.
2. When ready to cook, remove the pork from the fridge and preheat the air fryer oven to 360°F.
3. Spray the inner basket of the air fryer with cooking spray, then place the roast inside, skin side up, and spray it with cooking spray. Air fry for 50 minutes (~25 minutes per lb of meat) (covering it with foil to keep it from scorching if necessary) until the internal temperature has reached 140-145°F in the center of the thickest part.
4. Carefully remove the roast from the air fryer and place it on a cutting board. Cover it with aluminum foil and allow it to rest for 10 minutes before carving and serving.

Air Fryer Country Style Ribs
Servings: 5
Cooking Time: 20 Minutes

Ingredients:
- 2 lbs ribs country-style
- 1 tsp smoked paprika
- 1 1/2 tsp garlic powder
- 2 tsp ground black pepper
- 5 oz barbecue sauce

Directions:
1. Rinse the ribs and then pat them dry. Add the garlic powder, smoked paprika, and ground black seasoning to a small bowl and set aside.
2. Preheat the air fryer to 380 degrees Fahrenheit. Prepare the basket of the air fryer with nonstick cooking spray.

3. Rub the ribs with a small amount of the seasoning mixture.
4. Place the ribs in a single layer in the basket of the air fryer. Cook at 380 degrees for 20 minutes. Remove the basket and brush barbecue sauce onto the tops and sides of the ribs. Place back into the air fryer and cook for an additional 2 minutes. Check the internal temperature with a meat thermometer to ensure the pork has reached 145 degrees Fahrenheit.
5. Serve with your favorite sides.

NOTES

Store leftover country-style ribs in an airtight container in the refrigerator for up to 3 days.

This recipe was made using a Cosori 1700 watt 5.8 qt basket style air fryer. All air fryers can cook differently. It's always best to test a small batch before cooking the entire meal to decide if our air fryer requires more or less time.

Air Fryer Meatball Sub

Servings: 4

Ingredients:
- 2 large eggs
- 2 tsp. balsamic vinegar
- Kosher salt and pepper
- 1/3 c. panko
- 4 large cloves garlic (2 grated and 2 chopped)
- 1/4 c. freshly grated Parmesan cheese, plus more for serving
- 1/2 c. flat-leaf parsley, chopped
- 8 oz. sweet Italian sausage, casings removed
- 8 oz. ground beef
- 1 lb. cherry tomatoes
- 1 red chile, sliced
- 1 tbsp. olive oil
- 4 small hero rolls, split and toasted
- 6 tbsp. ricotta cheese
- Basil, for serving

Directions:
1. In a large bowl, whisk together eggs, vinegar and 1/2 teaspoon each salt and pepper. Stir in panko and let sit 1 minute. Stir in grated garlic and Parmesan, then parsley. Add sausage and beef and gently mix to combine.
2. Shape meat mixture into 20 balls (about 1 1/2 inches each) and place in a single layer on air-fryer rack (the balls can touch but should not be stacked; cook in batches if necessary). Air-fry meatballs at 400F for 5 minutes.
3. In a bowl, toss tomatoes, chile and chopped garlic with oil and 1/4 teaspoon each salt and pepper. Scatter over meatballs and continue air-frying until meatballs are cooked through, 5 to 6 minutes more.
4. Spread ricotta on toasted rolls, then top with meatballs, grated Parmesan, roasted tomatoes and chile and basil if desired.

Air Fryer Corn Ribs

Servings: 4
Cooking Time: 12 Minutes

Ingredients:
- 2 ears of corn fresh
- 1 Tablespoon butter unsalted
- 1/4 teaspoon garlic powder
- 1/4 teaspoon salt Kosher
- 1/2 teaspoon smoked paprika
- 1/2 teaspoon ground black pepper
- 1/2 teaspoon dried parsley
- fresh parsley for garnish

Directions:
1. Take each whole ear of corn, remove from the husk.
2. Rub cobs to remove the corn silks from in between the corn kernels and cut off the ends.
3. Place corn on the cobs in a microwave safe bowl covered with a damp paper towel and microwave for 2 minutes.
4. Let corn cobs cool for 5 minutes on a chopping board or until they are cool enough to touch.
5. Use a sharp knife and slice into the corn cobs: cut the corn in halves lengthwise, and

then cut halves into quarters, to make 4 pieces per cob of corn.
6. In a small bowl, combine butter, garlic powder, salt, paprika, black pepper and dried parsley.
7. Brush the corn ribs with the seasoning mixture, coating entire corn rib well.
8. In a single layer place the seasoned corn ribs into the air fryer basket.
9. Air fry at 400 degrees F for 12 minutes, flipping halfway through the cooking process.
10. Top with fresh parsley before serving.

NOTES
Optional Favorite Dipping Sauce: Ranch dressing, sour cream and chives, Carolina style bbq sauce, chipotle mayo or Greek yogurt with red pepper flakes.
Optional Additional Toppings: Lime wedges, fresh cilantro, fresh coriander or minced garlic butter.
Cooking Tips: Use a pastry brush to apply butter mixture to pieces of corn ribs. Cutting the corn into ribs makes it easier to eat especially for the little ones. For crispier corn cook for an additional 1-2 minutes.
Optional Additional Seasonings: Chili powder, lime juice, taco seasoning, chili oil, Elote seasoning, onion powder, cayenne pepper, chipotle powder or smoked salt.

Air Fryer Pork Chops In 9 Minutes

Servings: 4
Cooking Time: 9 Minutes

Ingredients:
- 4 medium pork chops boneless
- 1 tablespoon olive oil
- 2 teaspoons smoked paprika
- 2 teapoons cumin
- 1 teaspoon onion powder
- 1/2 teaspoon salt
- 1/2 teaspoon pepper

Directions:
1. Preheat the air fryer to 190C/375F.
2. Pat dry the boneless pork chops, then add into a bowl and rub the oil generously over them all.
3. Mix the spices in a bowl, then rub on both sides of the pork.
4. Place the pork chops in the air fryer basket and cook for 9 minutes, flipping halfway through.
5. Remove the pork from the air fryer and serve immediately.

Notes
TO STORE: Use air-tight containers to refrigerate the pork chops. They will keep well for up to five days.
TO FREEZE: Place leftovers in a ziplock bag and store them in the freezer for up to two months.
TO REHEAT: Either microwave the chops for 20-30 seconds or reheat in a non-stick pan until hot.

Air Fryer Brown Sugar And Honey Glazed Ham

Servings: 10
Cooking Time: 55 Minutes

Ingredients:
- 2-3 pounds (.9-1.36 kg) boneless, fully cooked ham
- BROWN SUGAR GLAZE
- 1/2 cup (110 g) brown sugar
- 1/4 cup (60 ml) honey
- 1/4 cup (60 ml) orange juice (or 1 orange juiced)
- 2 Tablespoons (60 ml) mustard (optional) or apple cider vinegar
- 1/4 teaspoon (1.25 ml) Cinnamon
- 1/4 teaspoon (1.25 ml) Clove
- black pepper , to taste
- Aluminum Foil
- 8" square Baking Pan

Directions:
1. Remove the ham from the fridge and allow to come up to room temperature, about 2 hours before cooking.
2. Make the Glaze: In a small saucepan or microwave safe bowl, combine the brown

sugar & honey glaze ingredients (brown sugar, honey, orange juice, optional mustard or apple cider vinegar, cinnamon, clove, and black pepper). Heat (can be done on the stovetop or in the microwave) and whisk until brown sugar is dissolved and glaze is well combined. Set aside.
3. If the ham has a netting, remove it from the ham. If ham is not pre-sliced, score the ham with shallow 1/2-inch criss-cross cuts.
4. For Basket Style Air Fryers: Line the air fryer basket with 2 pieces of long, overlapping foil sheets (see step-by step photos on website write up above). Lay the ham on top of the foil and then brush with some of the glaze to coat the ham. Close the foil over the ham and wrap tightly.
5. For Oven Style Air Fryers: Place the ham in an 8"x8" baking pan which fits in your air fryer (you may need to trim the edges of the ham to fit your pan and air fryer size). Brush with some of the glaze and close foil over the ham, wrapping tightly.
6. Air Fry at 340°F/170°C for 25 minutes. Open the foil and brush the ham with more glaze (make sure to reserve some glaze for finishing & serving). Close the foil tightly, and Air Fry again at 340°/170°C for 25 minutes.
7. After air frying for the 50 minutes, open up the foil again and now push the foil down around the edges of the ham if using the basket-style air fryer method. Create a boat with the foil that holds the juices and keeps the ham from drying out. If using the Oven Style Air Fryer method, just remove the foil from the 8"x8" pan.
8. Brush with a little more glaze and increase heat to Air Fry at 360°F/180°C for about 5 minutes, or until caramelized to your liking.
9. Let ham rest for 5 minutes before serving.
10. Optional serving: Combine the juices from the air fryer basket and the remaining glaze in a saucepan. Bring to a simmer and cook for about 5 minutes or until thickened.

Brush the glaze onto the ham when serving or serve in a bowl.

Air Fryer Pork Tenderloin
Servings: 2
Cooking Time: 22 Minutes

Ingredients:
- 1 pork tenderloin
- 1/2 cup olive oil
- 3 tablespoons soy sauce
- 2 cloves garlic, minced
- 2 tablespoons brown sugar
- 1 tablespoon dijon mustard
- salt and pepper, to taste

Directions:
1. Remove the pork tenderloin from its packaging and place aside.
2. Mix the olive oil, soy sauce, garlic, brown sugar, dijon mustard, and salt and pepper into a bowl then add to a Ziploc gallon bag.
3. Add the pork tenderloin to the bag, close it, and cover it with the marinade. Marinate the pork for 30 minutes, but up to 5 days while refrigerated.
4. Preheat the air fryer to 400 degrees.
5. Remove the pork tenderloin from the bag and place in the air fryer. Cook for 22 to 25 minutes flipping halfway through until it hits 145 degrees internally.
6. Let the air fryer pork tenderloin rest for at least 5 minutes, slice into medallions, and enjoy!

NOTES
HOW TO REHEAT PORK TENDERLOIN IN THE AIR FRYER:
Preheat your air fryer to 350 degrees.
Cook pork tenderloin for 3 to 5 minutes, until heated thoroughly and enjoy!
HOW TO COOK FROZEN PORK TENDERLOIN IN THE AIR FRYER:
Place frozen pork tenderloin in the air fryer and turn it to 330 degrees.
Cook the pork tenderloin for 33 to 38 minutes, until it reaches 145 degrees at its thickest point,

flipping and basting the marinade above halfway through cooking then enjoy!

Air Fryer Stuffed Peppers With Taco Meat

Servings: 4
Cooking Time: 15 Minutes

Ingredients:
- 2 bell peppers
- 1/2 pound (227 g) ground beef, pork, chicken or turkey
- 1/4 cup (60 g) tomato sauce
- 1 cup (113 g) shredded cheddar cheese, divided
- 1 teaspoon (5 ml) chili powder
- 1/2 teaspoon (2.5 ml) garlic powder
- 1/2 teaspoon (2.5 ml) ground cumin
- 1/2 teaspoon (2.5 ml) dried oregano
- 1/2 teaspoon (2.5 ml) salt, or to taste
- 1/4 teaspoon (1.25 ml) black pepper, or to taste
- olive oil or oil spray, for coating
- OPTIONAL TOPPINGS:
- green onions, salsa, guacamole, sour cream
- Oil Sprayer, optional

Directions:
1. In bowl, combine meat, tomato sauce, 1/2 cup cheese, chili powder, garlic powder, ground cumin, dried oregano, salt and pepper.
2. Cut bell peppers lengthwise and remove seeds.
3. Flip the bell peppers over and spray/brush outside of bell peppers with oil.
4. Stuff the pepper halves with the meat mixture. Spray tops of meat and peppers. Lay stuffed peppers inside air fryer basket/tray. If you have a small basket, you may have to cook in 2 batches.
5. Air Fry at 360°F/182°C for 12-16 minutes or until meat is cooked completely. Top the meat with remainder of cheese and cook one more minute to melt cheese.
6. Serve with your favorite toppings.
NOTES

COOKING TIPS: If bell peppers tilt and fall over, place a small crumpled piece of foil under the pepper as a base.
Cutting the peppers lengthwise will help meat cook quicker and all the way through. If. you cut them crosswise, you might need a couple more minutes of cooking time.

Air Fryer Meatballs

Servings: 4
Cooking Time: 20 Minutes

Ingredients:
- 1 lb ground beef
- 1/2 cup dried bread crumbs
- 1/2 cup grated Parmesan cheese
- 1/4 cup milk
- 2 cloves garlic minced
- 1/2 tsp Italian seasoning
- 3/4 tsp salt
- 1/4 tsp pepper

Directions:
1. Combine all ingredients in a bowl, then roll into 1 1/2 inch meatballs.
2. Put the meatballs into an air fryer basket in a single layer, without them touching.
3. Air fry the meatballs at 375F for 15 minutes.

Notes
If you want to serve meatballs with tomato sauce, heat prepared tomato sauce in a microwave and pour over cooked meatballs.
To make these meatballs low-carb, add more Parmesan cheese instead of bread crumbs.

Air Fryer Bacon Wrapped Jalapeños

Servings: 6
Cooking Time: 12 Minutes

Ingredients:
- 6 Jalapeño peppers
- 8 ounces cream cheese
- 4 ounces shredded cheddar cheese
- 6 pieces bacon

Directions:

1. Preheat the Air Fryer to 370 degrees Fahrenheit. Prepare the air fryer basket if needed with nonstick cooking spray, olive oil, or parchment paper.
2. Slice the jalapeño peppers in half, lengthwise. Use a small spoon to scoop the seeds and insides of each jalapeño half and then rinse.
3. Stuff each of the peppers with cream cheese. Top the cream cheese with shredded cheddar cheese.
4. Wrap each half of the stuffed jalapeño peppers with slices of bacon.
5. Place the bacon-wrapped jalapeño peppers in a single layer in the prepared air fryer basket.
6. Air Fry the peppers at 370 degrees Fahrenheit for 10-12 minutes or until the cream cheese filling has melted and the bacon is crispy.
7. Serve immediately.

NOTES

Are there flavor substitutions for jalapeno poppers?
Yes! You can add flavors to the cream cheese mixture and change things up easily. Consider adding in flavors such as onion powder, garlic powder, taco seasoning, or diced green onions.
Can I make bacon wrapped jalapeño poppers the day before?
Of course! You can follow the first few steps of making the jalapeno poppers and then store them in an airtight container in the refrigerator. When you're ready to cook, remove them from the refrigerator and cook as instructed at 370 degrees Fahrenheit for 10-12 minutes.
NOTE: This recipe for air fryer bacon wrapped jalapeno poppers was made using the 5.8qt Cosori Air Fryer. If you're using a different type of air fryer, you may need to adjust the cooking time up or down a minute or two to ensure your poppers cook accordingly.

Air Fryer Boneless Pork Chops

Servings: 2 - 2

Ingredients:
- 2 8 oz boneless pork chops (1.25" thick)
- Kosher salt and freshly ground black pepper
- 2 tsp. pork rub (optional)

Directions:
1. Set air fryer to 400F and preheat 3 to 4 minutes. Pat pork chops dry, and season both sides with salt and pepper and/or a spice rub.
2. Place pork chops into heated air fryer and cook, 6 minutes.
3. Flip chops and cook until internal temperature on an instant read thermometer reads 135F-145F, 5-8 minutes. If it's not warm enough, continue cooking, checking every 2-3 minutes, until cooked through.
4. Cover chops with a tent of aluminum foil and let rest 5 minutes, to allow chops to reabsorb juices, before slicing and eating.

Air Fryer Beef & Broccoli Noodle Stir Fry

Servings: 2
Cooking Time: 10 Minutes

Ingredients:
- 300g pack frying steak
- 1/4 x 1 tsp bicarbonate of soda
- 3 clove/s cloves garlic, finely grated
- 30g ginger, finely grated
- 2 tbsp Shaoxing rice wine (or dry sherry)
- 2 tbsp light soy sauce
- 1/2 x 1 tsp caster sugar
- 1/2 x 1 tsp freshly ground black peppercorns
- 2 tbsp Vegetable oil
- 210g pack Sweet and Tender Stir Fry Mix
- 1/2 x 1 tsp sesame oil
- 1 tbsp dark soy sauce
- 275g pack fresh medium egg noodles

Directions:
1. Trim the steaks and cut into 0.5cm slices at an angle against the grain. Using the back

of your knife, spread each piece even more thinly across the chopping board. Transfer to a medium bowl with a pinch of salt, the bicarbonate of soda, garlic, ginger, Shaoxing rice wine, light soy sauce, sugar, ground pepper and 1 tbsp water. Chill for at least 30 minutes (ideally 2 hours and up to 24 hours ahead).

2. Put the marinated beef in the air-fryer basket without the rack. Toss with the vegetable oil and air-fry at 200ºC for 6-8 minutes, stirring halfway, until tender and just cooked through with some crispy edges. Add the stir fry mix, sesame oil and dark soy sauce, then air-fry for a further 3 minutes until the veg is tender. Stir through the noodles and cook for a final 2 minutes. Serve immediately.

Cook's tip
Customer safety tips
Follow manufacturer's instructions and advice for specific foods
Pre-heat the air fryer to the correct temperature
If cooking different foods together, be aware that they may require different times and temperatures
Spread food evenly – do not overcrowd pan/chamber
Turn food midway through cooking
Check food is piping/steaming hot and cooked all the way through
Aim for golden colouring – do not overcook

Air Fryer Brown Sugar Pork Chops

Servings: 4
Cooking Time: 12 Minutes

Ingredients:
- 4 boneless center cut pork chops 1 ½ – 2 inches thick
- 2 tablespoons brown sugar
- 1 tablespoon paprika
- 1 ½ teaspoons salt
- 1 ½ teaspoons fresh ground black pepper
- 1 teaspoon ground mustard
- ½ teaspoon onion powder
- ¼ teaspoon garlic powder
- 2 tablespoons olive oil

Directions:
1. Preheat air fryer to 400°F on bake.
2. Pat pork chops dry with a paper towel.
3. In a small bowl, mix together all the dry ingredients.
4. Coat the pork chops with olive oil and rub in the mixture.
5. Cook pork chops for 12 minutes, flipping pork chops over after 6 minutes.

Notes
Leftover pork chops will keep in an airtight container in the refrigerator for up to 4 days.

Air Fryer Bacon Wrapped Brussel Sprouts

Servings: 4
Cooking Time: 13 Minutes

Ingredients:
- 8 slices bacon regular and sliced in half
- 16 small Brussels sprouts
- ¼ cup brown sugar

Directions:
1. Wrap one slice of halved bacon around each brussels sprout, seal with a toothpick if necessary. Repeat until all sprouts have been wrapped.
2. In a large glass bowl, toss wrapped sprouts with brown sugar, until they are well coated.
3. Place in the air fryer basket, without stacking or overlapping.
4. Air Fry at 380 degrees F for 13-16 minutes, until bacon is crispy.

NOTES
Variations
Change up the flavor of bacon - You can use salty bacon, crispy bacon, thick cut bacon, or any piece of bacon or strip of bacon that you want. Maple bacon sounds like some pretty good strips of bacon to add to this easy recipe!
Add toppings - Let's be truthful here and say that toppings are always a crowd-pleaser. Drizzling some olive oil with salt and black

pepper on top of this delicious appetizer adds taste in an easy way.

You can add soy sauce to these tender brussels sprouts after they are done cooking, or add some sweetness with a drizzle of maple syrup!

Air Fryer Easter Pork Roast

Servings: 4
Cooking Time: 2 Hours 10 Minutes

Ingredients:
- 1 x Pork loin joint
- 1 x Pack of green beans
- 1x Head of broccoli
- 1 x Apple
- 4x Pieces of streaky smoked bacon
- 1x Tinned New Potatoes
- 2x Large Carrots
- 4x Yorkshire Puddings

Directions:
1. Season the pork with salt & pepper. Place pork into drawer 1 of the air fryer at 160 for 1hr 20 mins.
2. Whilst the pork is cooking trim both ends of the green beans, cut the broccoli into florets and peel the carrots and cut into 2cm chunks. Toss all prepared vegetables in a little oil, salt & pepper and set aside.
3. ¼ the apple and cut off the core, wrap with 1 piece of streaky bacon. Pop in the fridge until later on.
4. After 1 hour put the carrots into drawer 2 at 160 and cook for 20 mins.
5. Remove the pork, check it is cooked all the way through and leave to rest on a plate covered loosely with foil.
6. Add the green beans and the broccoli to drawer 2 with the carrots, increase the temp to 200 and cook for 10 mins.
7. Place the potatoes into drawer 1 at 200 and cook for 10 mins.
8. Take the apple pieces out of the fridge and pop them into drawer 1 with the potatoes and cook for a further 10 mins.
9. While plating all the ingredients place the Yorkshires into an empty drawer and cook for 4 mins at 200.
10. Serve with gravy and enjoy! Why not use any leftovers and create delicious pork sandwiches the next day or even try a Leftover Yorkshire Pudding Wrap!

Air Fryer Korean-inspired Pork Tenderloin Lettuce Wraps

Servings: 2-4

Ingredients:
- 1 lb. pork tenderloin
- 3/4 tsp. kosher salt
- 1/4 c. gochujang (Korean hot pepper paste)
- 1 clove garlic, finely grated
- 2 tbsp. honey
- 1 tbsp. toasted sesame oil
- 1/4 tsp. finely grated fresh ginger
- 1 tbsp. unseasoned rice vinegar
- Olive oil cooking spray
- 1 head of Bibb or butter lettuce, leaves separated
- Sliced cucumber, sliced scallions, and cooked rice, for serving

Directions:
1. Cut pork in half crosswise; season all over with salt.
2. In a medium bowl, combine gochujang, garlic, honey, oil, and ginger. Transfer 1/4 cup gochujang mixture to a small bowl and stir in vinegar; set aside for serving. Add pork to bowl with remaining sauce and toss to coat.
3. Lightly coat an air-fryer basket with cooking spray. Place pork in basket and cook at 350°, turning occasionally, until pork is golden brown and an instant-read thermometer inserted into thickest part registers 140°, 16 to 19 minutes. Let rest about 10 minutes before slicing.
4. Place pork in lettuce leaves, along with cucumber, scallions, and rice. Serve with reserved sauce alongside.

Air Fryer Bacon Wrapped Dates

Servings: 3
Cooking Time: 10 Minutes

Ingredients:
- 6 pieces of bacon
- 4 ounces cream cheese
- 1 tsp cinnamon
- 18 Medjool pitted dates

Directions:
1. Slice bacon pieces into halves. Set aside.
2. Slice open the tops of the dates and remove the pits if not already pitted.
3. In a small bowl, mix together the cream cheese and cinnamon.
4. Carefully spoon ½ teaspoon of the cinnamon and cream cheese mixture into each date.
5. Wrap each date with a piece of the bacon, and carefully secure the bacon with a toothpick if needed.
6. Air fry the bacon-wrapped dates at 350 degrees Fahrenheit for 10 minutes or until the bacon is cooked fully.
7. Carefully remove the stuffed dates from the air fryer and serve.

NOTES

These are so simple to serve! You can add them to a charcuterie board for a fun treat or serve them up on a platter at your next party.

I do think that this delicious appetizer is best eaten fresh, but you can always store it for later. Let the stuffed date cool down all the way, and then add any leftovers to an airtight container. Place the container in the fridge and keep it cool. Eat within 2 days for the best flavor.

Air Fryer Grilled Ham And Cheese

Servings: 4
Cooking Time: 7 Minutes

Ingredients:
- 2 tablespoons mayonnaise
- 8 slices white bread
- 2 tablespoons Dijon mustard
- 8 slices deli ham
- 4 large slices Swiss cheese
- 8 dill pickle slices
- cooking spray

Directions:
1. Spread mayonnaise on one side of each slice of bread. With mayo side down, lightly spread 4 slices of bread with Dijon mustard, evenly top each with Swiss cheese, ham slices, folded to fit, and pickle slices. Place the remaining 4 bread slices on the sandwiches, mayo side up, and lightly press sandwiches to close.
2. Preheat the air fryer to 380 degrees F (193 degrees C). Spray the air fryer basket with cooking spray or line with a parchment liner.
3. Place sandwiches in the air fryer basket in a single layer, leaving some space around them. You may have to cook the sandwiches in batches, depending on the size of your fryer.
4. Cook until sandwiches begin to brown, 3 to 4 minutes. Flip, and cook until cheese has melted and sandwiches are golden brown, 2 to 3 minutes more. Slice sandwiches in half and serve warm.

Note:

Mayonnaise is the only thing I use these days on grilled sandwiches. It's always ready, spreads easily, browns beautifully, and has no mayo flavor. But you can use butter, if you prefer. Air fryer cooking times may vary depending on the brand and size. So watch your sandwiches closely, especially toward the end of cooking.

Air Fryer Crispy Chilli Beef

Servings: 2
Cooking Time: 15 Minutes

Ingredients:
- 250g thin-cut minute steak, thinly sliced into strips
- 2 tbsp cornflour
- 2 tbsp vegetable oil, plus a drizzle
- 2 garlic cloves, crushed
- thumb-sized piece of ginger, peeled and cut into matchsticks
- 1 red chilli, thinly sliced
- 1 red pepper, cut into chunks
- 4 spring onions, sliced, green and white parts separated
- 4 tbsp rice wine vinegar or white wine vinegar
- 1 tbsp soy sauce
- 2 tbsp sweet chilli sauce
- 2 tbsp tomato ketchup
- For the marinade
- ? tsp Chinese five-spice powder
- 2 tsp soy sauce
- 1 tsp sesame oil
- 1 tsp caster sugar

Directions:
1. First, combine the marinade ingredients in a bowl. Add the steak strips and toss to coat. Leave in the fridge for up to 24 hrs if you can, or carry on to step 2.
2. Sprinkle the cornflour over the steak and mix until each piece is coated in a floury paste. Pull the strips apart and arrange over a plate. Drizzle each piece of steak with a little oil. Heat the air fryer to 220C if it has a preheat setting.
3. Carefully put the beef on the cooking rack in the air fryer, cook for 6 mins, then turn and cook for another 4-6 mins until crispy.
4. Meanwhile, heat 2 tbsp vegetable oil in a wok over a high heat and stir-fry the garlic, ginger, chilli, pepper and white ends of the spring onions for 2-3 mins until the pepper softens. Be careful not to burn the ginger and garlic. Add the vinegar, soy, sweet chilli sauce and tomato ketchup, mix well and cook for another minute until bubbling.
5. Tip the beef into the wok and toss through the sauce. Continue cooking for another minute until piping hot, then serve scattered with the spring onion greens and a little extra sauce on the side.

Air Fryer Bbq Chops

Ingredients:
- 500g chops washed and cleaned, pat dry
- 1 teaspoon crushed garlic
- 1/2 teaspoon crushed green chilli
- 1/2 teaspoon salt
- 1/2 teaspoon onion powder
- 1/2 teaspoon garlic powder
- 1/4 cup spare rib marinade
- 1/4 cup BBQ sauce

Directions:
1. Marinate chops in above ingredients, allow to marinate overnight. In drawer 1 add in your chops, set the air fryer on air-fry, 180 degrees celsius for 20 minutes. On turn food prompt baste chops with left over marinate.
2. In drawer 2, place your pre-cooked garlic bread, air-fry for 2 minutes on 180 degrees celsius, to melt butter and bread to soften. And then press the synch finish button. This feature allows both drawers to finish cooking at the same time.
3. Serve immediately with all your favourite braai sides, enjoy.

SANDWICHES & BURGERS RECIPES

Keto Friendly Game Day Burgers

Ingredients:
- Mini Beef Burgers:
- 1.5 pounds ground beef
- 1/4 cup onion, diced
- 1 tsp salt
- 1/4 tsp pepper
- 1 tsp brown Mustard
- Low Carb Sauce:
- 1/2 cup mayonnaise
- 1 tsp white wine vinegar
- 1 tsp paprika
- 1 tsp garlic powder
- 1 tsp onion powder
- 4 tbsp dill pickle relish

Directions:
1. Using your hands mix together the beef, onion, salt, pepper, and brown sugar (optional.)
2. Form into 15-20 mini balls.
3. Cook in your air fryer, flipping half way to your desired doneness, 7-8 minutes at 390 degrees.
4. While the burgers are cooking, mix your mayonnaise, white vinegar, paprika, garlic powder, onion powder, and dill pickle relish together. Set to the side.
5. Place each burger on a skewer with cheese, lettuce, pickles, and the special sauce.
6. Enjoy!

Air Fryer Hamburgers

Servings: 4
Cooking Time: 8 Minutes

Ingredients:
- 1-pound ground beef, thawed (preferably 80/20)
- 1 clove garlic, minced
- 1/2 teaspoon salt
- 1/4 teaspoon pepper

Directions:
1. Preheat air fryer to 360 degrees.
2. Mix together the ground beef, minced garlic, salt, and pepper with your hands.
3. Form ground beef into 4 patties and press them down with the back of a pie plate to make them evenly flat.
4. Place hamburgers in a single layer inside the air fryer.
5. Cook for 8-12 minutes, flipping halfway through cooking for medium-well hamburgers.*
6. Carefully remove hamburgers from the air fryer,** place onto hamburger buns (if using), and add desired toppings.

NOTES
*thicker hamburgers may take longer to cook if not pressed down properly
** if making cheeseburgers, place a piece of cheese on each burger in the air fryer, turn the air fryer off, and let the burgers sit in the air fryer for 1 to 2 minutes until melted

Air Fried Crispy Chicken Sandwiches

Servings: 4

Ingredients:
- 2 large chicken breasts, cut in half and pounded to an even thickness
- 1 cup buttermilk
- 1 tablespoon kosher salt or 1 teaspoon table salt
- ¾ cup panko breadcrumbs
- ½ cup all-purpose flour
- ½ teaspoon salt
- ¼ teaspoon dried oregano
- ½ teaspoon paprika
- ¼ teaspoon garlic powder
- ¼ teaspoon dried thyme
- ¼ teaspoon ground ginger
- ½ teaspoon ground black pepper
- Oil spray
- 4 brioche burger buns
- Assorted toppings such as lettuce, tomato, onions and additional condiments

Directions:
1. Place the chicken breasts in a zipper top bag and pour in buttermilk and salt. Squeeze the air out and seal the bag. Marinate in the refrigerator for at least an hour or preferably overnight.
2. In a shallow bowl combine the panko breadcrumbs, flour and spices.
3. Remove the chicken breasts from the buttermilk. Remove excess buttermilk and dredge in the breadcrumb mixture.
4. Arrange the chicken breasts in one layer on a parchment-lined baking sheet, thoroughly coating chicken with oil spray on both sides.
5. Air Fry at 375°F for 20 – 25 minutes or until internal temperature reads 165°F and the chicken breasts are golden brown and crispy. For more even cooking, flip the chicken halfway through and spray with more oil if desired.
6. Serve chicken sandwiches on toasted brioche buns with lettuce, tomatoes, red onion and other favorite condiments.

Air Fryer Grilled Cheese Sandwich
Servings: 2
Cooking Time: 7 Minutes

Ingredients:
- 8 slices white bread
- 1 tablespoon butter
- 4 slices cheese

Directions:
1. Spread a light layer of the butter on one side of each piece of bread.
2. Place the buttered side down in the air fryer basket.
3. Cover the slice of bread with a piece of cheese. Then top the cheese with another slice of bread, with the buttered side up.
4. Air Fry at 370 degrees F for 3-5 minutes. Then flip, and air fry for 2-3 additional minutes, until bread reaches desired crispness.

NOTES

Make this a heartier meal by adding a few slices of bacon to the sandwich, avocado slices, or on inside of slices, spread bread with pesto sauce before adding cheese.

Depending on the type of bread you use, you may want to adjust the cook times. For softer bread, or French Bread, air fry until it reaches your desired crispness.

Air Fryer Bacon, Egg And Cheese Biscuit Breakfast Sandwiches
Servings: 8

Ingredients:
- 1 can (16.3 oz) refrigerated Pillsbury™ Grands!™ Southern Homestyle Original Biscuits (8 Count)
- 6 eggs
- 1/4 teaspoon salt
- 1/8 teaspoon pepper, if desired
- 1 tablespoon butter
- 8 slices cooked bacon, cut in half crosswise
- 8 slices (3/4 oz each) American cheese

Directions:
1. Spray bottom of air fryer basket with cooking spray. Separate dough into 8 biscuits. Place 4 biscuits in air fryer basket, spacing apart.
2. Set air fryer to 330°F; cook 6 minutes. Using tongs or spatula, turn over each biscuit. Cook 4 to 5 minutes or until biscuits are deep golden brown and cooked through. Remove from air fryer; cover loosely with foil to keep warm while cooking second batch. Cook remaining biscuits as directed above.
3. Meanwhile, in medium bowl, beat eggs, salt and pepper thoroughly with fork or whisk until well mixed. In 10-inch skillet, heat butter over medium heat just until butter begins to sizzle. Pour egg mixture into skillet. Cook until set, stirring occasionally.
4. To serve, split warm biscuits; top bottom half of each with scrambled eggs, bacon and cheese. Cover with top halves of biscuits.

Air Fryer Frozen Burger

Servings: 2
Cooking Time: 15 Minutes

Ingredients:
- 2 frozen burger patties

Directions:
1. Place frozen burgers in a single layer in the basket of the air fryer.
2. Air fry the burgers at 350 degrees Fahrenheit for 15 minutes, flipping the burgers halfway through cook time.
3. If desired, add sliced cheese during the last minute of cooking time.
4. Carefully remove the burgers from the air fryer and serve them with your favorite toppings.

NOTES
If adding cheese, top with sliced cheese during the last minute of cook time.
Serve bunless for a healthier burger.

Air Fryer Chicken Burgers

Servings: 4
Cooking Time: 10 Minutes

Ingredients:
- 1 pound ground chicken
- 1 large egg
- 1 cup mozzarella cheese shredded
- 1/2 cup onion finely chopped
- 1/2 cup panko breadcrumbs
- 1 teaspoon minced garlic
- 1/2 teaspoon kosher salt
- 1/4 teaspoon ground black pepper

Directions:
1. Preheat air fryer to 365 degrees F.
2. In a large bowl, combine the chicken, egg, cheese, onion, panko crumbs, garlic, salt and pepper. Mix chicken mixture together with your hands until fully combined.
3. Divide the chicken mixture into 4 equal parts and shape them into 5-inch diameter burgers.
4. Spray the air fryer basket with non-stick cooking spray and place the chicken patties in air fryer in a single layer.
5. Air fry the chicken burgers at 365 degrees F for 8-10 minutes or until cooked through, depending on the thickness of the patties.
6. Use a meat thermometer to confirm internal temperature of burger patties which should be a safe temperature of 165 degrees F.
7. Allow chicken burgers to cool for a couple of minutes then carefully remove them from the basket.
8. Serve while hot or let them continue to rest on a baking rack.

NOTES
Optional Additional Favorite Sauces: BBQ sauce, mustard yogurt sauce, chili sauce, ketchup, spicy sriracha sauce (based on your spice level), honey mustard, marinara sauce, relish or a sweet and spicy pickle.

Optional Favorite Toppings: Shredded lettuce, slice of tomato, raw or caramelized onions, sundried tomato strips, bacon, avocado, pepper jack cheese, American cheese or shredded cheese.

Cooking Tips: Use a silicone mat to make it an easy clean up and prevent food sticking to your basket. For crispy chicken patties brush a little olive oil on the patties prior to placing them in your air fryer.

I make this recipe in my Cosori 5.8 qt. air fryer. Depending on your air fryer, size and wattages, your cooking time may need to be adjusted 1-2 minutes.

Greek Lamb Burgers With Baked Eggplant Fries

Servings: 4

Ingredients:
- Nonstick cooking spray
- 1 pound ground lamb
- 2 ounces feta cheese, crumbled (about ½ cup)
- ½ cup grated red onion (from 1 small onion), divided

- 1 ½ tablespoon olive oil, divided
- 2 ½ teaspoons kosher salt, divided
- ¾ teaspoon freshly ground black pepper, divided
- 1 ½ cups panko
- 2 large egg whites
- 1 medium eggplant, cut into ½-by-1-by-2-in. wedges
- ½ cup grated English cucumber (from ½ cucumber)
- 1 cup plain whole-milk Greek yogurt
- 2 teaspoons fresh lemon juice (from 1 lemon)
- Hamburger buns and lettuce, for serving

Directions:
1. Preheat oven to 425°F. Lightly coat a rimmed baking sheet with cooking spray. Stir together lamb, cheese, ¼ cup onion, 1 tablespoon oil, 1 teaspoon salt, and ½ teaspoon pepper in a bowl until just combined; shape into 4 patties.
2. Combine panko and remaining 1½ teaspoons salt in a large ziplock plastic bag. Whisk egg whites in a large bowl until foamy. Dip eggplant wedges, 1 at a time, in egg whites and transfer to bag with panko. Once all eggplant has been added to bag, seal and shake well to coat. Arrange eggplant in an even layer on prepared baking sheet and coat generously with cooking spray. Bake until golden brown, about 20 minutes, flipping halfway through.
3. Meanwhile, heat remaining ½ tablespoon oil in a large nonstick skillet over medium-high. Add lamb patties and cook, flipping once, until browned, about 4 minutes per side for medium.
4. Place cucumber and remaining ¼ cup onion on a paper towel. Squeeze gently to release liquid. Transfer to a small bowl and stir in yogurt, lemon juice, and remaining ¼ teaspoon pepper.
5. Place patties on buns with lettuce and yogurt sauce. Serve with eggplant fries and remaining yogurt sauce.

Air Fryer Biscuit Egg Sandwiches
Servings: 4

Ingredients:
- Deselect All
- Nonstick cooking spray, for the molds
- 4 large eggs
- Kosher salt
- 4 thin slices deli ham
- One 16.3-ounce tube refrigerated flaky biscuit dough, such as Pillsbury
- Hot sauce, for serving

Directions:
1. Special equipment: 4 silicone baking cups, 6-quart air fryer
2. Spray 4 silicone baking cups with nonstick spray. Transfer the cups to the basket of a 6-quart air fryer.
3. Whisk together the eggs in a large glass measuring cup until no white streaks remain. Season with 1/2 teaspoon salt. Divide the eggs among the baking cups. Insert a piece of ham into each cup, crumpling it to make it fit (some of the ham should stick out above the surface of the eggs).
4. Tear off 4 biscuits from the tube of dough. Place each biscuit in the basket of the air fryer in a single layer. Set the air fryer to 300 degrees F and cook for 10 minutes. The biscuits should be golden brown; transfer to a cutting board.
5. Gently lift each egg muffin from its mold so you can see if it's set. If there's no liquid egg on the bottom, transfer the mold to the cutting board. If there is liquid egg on the bottom, cook for up to 1 minute more.
6. Slice each biscuit in half crosswise. Remove the egg muffins from the molds and slice in half crosswise. Arrange the two egg halves on each bottom biscuit, drizzle with plenty of hot sauce and sandwich with the top biscuit.

Air Fryer Burgers From Frozen Patties

Servings: 4
Cooking Time: 15 Minutes

Ingredients:
- 4 frozen raw beef patties, usually sold as either 1/4 lb.(113g) or 1/3 lb.(150g)
- salt, to taste if needed
- Lots of black pepper
- oil spray, for coating
- BURGER ASSEMBLY:
- 4 Buns, + optional cheese, pickles, lettuce, onion, tomato, avocado, cooked bacon etc.
- EQUIPMENT
- Air Fryer
- Instant Read Thermometer (optional)

Directions:
1. Spray both sides of frozen burger patties with oil. Season with salt and pepper if needed. Spray the air fryer basket with oil and place the patties in the basket in a single layer. Cook in batches if needed.
2. For 1/4 lb. frozen burger patties: Air Fry at 360°F/180°C for a total of about 8-12 minutes. After the first 6 minutes flip the patties and continue to Air Frying at 360°F/180°C for another 2-6 minutes or until it's cooked to your preferred doneness. The internal temperature should be 160°F/71°C.
3. For 1/3 lb. frozen burger patties: Air Fry at 360°F/180°C for a total of about 12-16 minutes. After the first 10 minutes flip the patties and continue to Air Frying at 360°F/180°C for another 2-6 minutes or until it's cooked to your preferred doneness. The internal temperature should be 160°F/71°C.
4. For Cheeseburgers: add the slices of cheese on top of the cooked patties. Air fry at 360°F/180°C for about 30 seconds to 1 minute to melt the cheese.
5. Cover the patties and let rest for 3 minutes. Warm the buns in the air fryer at 380°F/193°C for about 3 minutes while patties are resting. Serve on buns, topped with your favorite burger toppings.

FISH & SEAFOOD RECIPES

Air Fryer Tuna Patties

Servings: 10
Cooking Time: 10 Minutes

Ingredients:
- 15 ounces (425 g) canned albacore tuna, drained or 1 pound (454g) fresh tuna, diced
- 2-3 large eggs *see note above
- zest of 1 medium lemon
- 1 Tablespoon (15 ml) lemon juice
- 1/2 cup (55 g) bread crumbs or crushed pork rinds for keto/low carb
- 3 Tablespoons (45 ml) grated parmesan cheese
- 1 stalk celery, finely chopped
- 3 Tablespoons (45 ml) minced onion
- 1/2 teaspoon (2.5 ml) garlic powder
- 1/2 teaspoon (2.5 ml) dried herbs (oregano, dill, basil, thyme or any combo)
- 1/4 teaspoon (1.25 ml) Kosher salt, or to taste
- fresh cracked black pepper
- optional for serving - ranch, tarter sauce, mayo, lemon slices
- EQUIPMENT
- Air Fryer
- Air Fryer Parchment Paper optional
- Perforated Silicone Mats optional
- Oil Sprayer optional

Directions:
1. In a medium bowl, combine the eggs, lemon zest, lemon juice, bread crumbs, parmesan cheese, celery, onion, garlic powder, dried herbs, salt and pepper. Stir to make sure everything is combined. Gently fold in the tuna until just combined.
2. Try to keep all patties same size and thickness for even cooking. Scoop 1/4 cup of mixture, and shape into patties about 3-inches wide x 1/2-inch thick and lay inside basket. Makes about 10 patties.
3. If patties are too soft to handle, chill them for at about 1 hour or until firm. This will make them easier to handle during cooking. Spray or brush top of patties with oil.
4. If you have air fryer perforated baking paper or perforated silicone mats, they are great for this recipe. Lay perforated air fryer baking paper or perforated silicone mat inside base of air fryer. Lightly spray the paper or mat. (if not you don't have the liners, spray enough olive oil spray at the base of the air fryer basket to make sure the patties do not stick)
5. Air Fry at 360°F for 6 minutes. Flip the patties and spray the tops again with oil. Continue to Air Fry for another 3-5 minutes or until cooked to your preference.
6. Serve with your favorite sauce and lemon slices.

NOTES
Easy substitutions: Fresh herbs for the dried herbs. Shallots or green onions for the onions.

Air Fryer Scallops

Servings: 4
Cooking Time: 5 Minutes

Ingredients:
- 1/2 lb scallops
- 1/2 teaspoon salt
- 1/4 teaspoon pepper
- 2 tablespoons butter divided
- 1/4 cup parsley finely chopped
- 1/2 small lemon sliced

Directions:
1. Pat dry the scallops and then sprinkle with salt and pepper. Brush one tablespoon of butter over the scallops.
2. Generously grease an air fryer basket with cooking spray and add a single layer of scallops.
3. Air fry at 200C/400 for 5-7 minutes, flipping halfway through.
4. Remove them from the air fryer basket, and brush more butter on them. Sprinkle with

finely chopped parsley and serve with sliced lemon.

Notes

TO STORE: Place leftover scallops in a shallow container and store them in the refrigerator for up to two days.

TO FREEZE: Once the scallops have cooled to room temperature, place them in a shallow container and store them in the freezer for up to two months.

TO REHEAT: Reheat in the air fryer or microwave until warm.

Frozen Shrimp In The Air Fryer

Servings: 4
Cooking Time: 7 Minutes

Ingredients:
- 1 pound frozen cooked large shrimp
- 1 tablespoon unsalted butter, melted
- 1 tablespoon Old Bay seasoning
- ½ tablespoon lemon juice
- 1 teaspoon minced garlic

Directions:
1. Heat air fryer to 350 degrees F.
2. Break apart frozen shrimp and place the shrimp, butter, Old Bay seasoning, lemon juice, and garlic in a large bowl. Stir to combine and coat all of the shrimp.
3. In a single layer lay your shrimp (about ½ a pound per batch) and cook for 6 to 7 minutes until fully heated.

Fish 'n' Chips

Servings: 4

Ingredients:
- For the chips
- 700g King Edward or Maris Piper potatoes
- 2 tbsp sunflower oil
- Sea salt
- 2 tsp semolina (optional)
- lemon wedges and parsley to garnish
- For the fish
- 2 slices stale bread, crusts removed and torn into pieces
- 1 garlic clove
- 1 zest of lemon
- 5g fresh parsley, leaves and stalks
- sea salt and pepper to taste
- 1 x 120g chunky thick skinless cod fillets, pat dry
- 2 tbsp oil
- COOKING MODE
- When entering cooking mode - We will enable your screen to stay 'always on' to avoid any unnecessary interruptions whilst you cook!

Directions:
1. Peel potatoes and cut into 5cm thick chips. Place in a bowl, cover with water and allow to soak for 30 minutes to remove excess starch. Rinse and pat potatoes dry.
2. In a clean bowl, add chips, oil, salt and semolina. Toss together to make sure the chips are coated. Insert crisper plates into both drawers and add the chips to Zone 1 drawer.
3. Place bread, garlic, lemon, parsley and seasoning into a food processor. Whizz until you have fine breadcrumbs. Add oil and pulse until mixed. Spoon breadcrumb topping onto cod. Press topping on with the back of spoon. Spray Zone 2 drawer and carefully place topped cod into drawer.
4. Select Zone 1, turn the dial to select AIR FRY, set temperature to 200°C, and set time to 26 minutes. Select Zone 2 and turn the dial to select ROAST, set temperature to 170°C and set time to 14 minutes. Select SYNC. Press the dial to begin cooking.
5. After 10 minutes, shake Zone 1 drawer, shake again after 15 and 20 minutes. Check at 24 minutes if cooked enough.
6. When cooking time is complete, remove fish and chips and serve with tartar sauce and mushy peas.

Air Fryer Blackened Mahi Mahi

Servings: 4
Cooking Time: 9 Minutes

Ingredients:
- 4 mahi mahi fillets 3-4 oz each
- 2 tablespoons olive oil
- 3 tablespoons blackening seasoning

Directions:
1. Preheat air fryer to 400°F.
2. Pat fillets dry and generously rub with olive oil then coat them with blackening seasoning.
3. Place fillets in the air fryer basket and cook for 7-9 minutes.
4. Fish should reach 145°F internally and be opaque and flaky.

Notes
For the best crispy crust, preheat the air fryer first. If cooking in batches, keep warm in the oven and broil before serving.
Cooking time can vary with the thickness of the fish. Check the temperature of the fish early to ensure it doesn't overcook.
Serving Suggestion: Serve with fruit salsa like pineapple salsa or the quick bell pepper salsa below.
Quick Bell Pepper Salsa (optional): Dice one Roma tomato, half a bell pepper, and two tablespoons of red onion. Season with a squeeze of lime juice, a teaspoon of olive oil, and salt and pepper. Add a sprinkle of cilantro.

Air Fryer Breaded Shrimp

Servings: 4
Cooking Time: 8 Minutes

Ingredients:
- 1 pound large raw shrimp peeled and deveined (I use 31/40 size)
- 1 cup Italian Breadcrumbs
- ¼ cup grated Parmesan cheese
- 1/2 cup all purpose flour
- 1/3 cup water
- 1/2 tsp dried parsley flakes
- 1/2 tsp paprika
- ½ tsp salt
- ¼ tsp ground black pepper
- 1 large egg

Directions:
1. In a shallow bowl, add breadcrumbs, parmesan cheese, parsley flakes, paprika, salt and pepper. Stir with a fork to combine ingredients.
2. In another large bowl, add the flour, egg, and water. Stir together to make a liquid batter.
3. Toss shrimp with the flour and egg batter, until they are coated on both sides.
4. Dredge each piece of shrimp in the panko mixture, coating both sides.
5. Lightly spray the air fryer basket, and place each shrimp into the basket, without stacking or overlapping.
6. Lightly spritz the coated shrimp with olive oil and then place shrimp in the air fryer basket. Air Fry at 380 degrees F for 8-10 minutes, flipping shrimp halfway through air frying.

NOTES
Variations
Use panko breadcrumbs - Instead of using regular bread crumbs, you can use Panko bread crumbs.
Change the seasoning - Use Old Bay seasoning, lemon pepper, red pepper flakes, Cajun seasoning, and any other flavors that you want to add to this shrimp recipe. The flavors take to the larger shrimp easily.
Make air fryer frozen shrimp - If you want to cook tender seafood, you can cook frozen shrimp in the air fryer as well. Just add them in a single layer in the basket of the air fryer.

Air Fryer Fish & Chips

Servings: 2
Cooking Time: 25 Minutes

Ingredients:
- Chips:
- 2 large potatoes, scrubbed, dried & sliced into chunky chips
- 1 Tbsp olive oil

- Salt, to taste
- Fish:
- 2 x 200g kingklip fillets (or similar firm white fish)
- 1 cup flour
- 1 XL egg, whisked
- ½ cup panko breadcrumbs
- ½ tsp sweet paprika
- ½ tsp garlic powder
- Salt and pepper, to taste
- Tartar sauce:
- 200ml mayonnaise
- 3 Tbsp baby capers, roughly chopped
- 3 Tbsp gherkins, finely minced
- 2 Tbsp fresh parsley, finely minced
- 1 Tbsp lemon zest
- 1 Tbsp lemon juice
- Lemon wedges, to serve

Directions:
1. In a bowl combine the potatoes, olive oil and salt.
2. Toss well to coat.
3. Spread out on one of the slotted Vortex Oven baking trays.
4. Set the Vortex Oven to Air Fry for 10 min at 202°C.
5. Once preheated add the chips in the bottom half of the oven, above the solid baking tray.
6. Place flour and whisked egg in 2 shallow bowls.
7. In a third shallow bowl combine the panko breadcrumbs, paprika, garlic powder and a little salt and pepper. Mix.
8. Season the fish fillets with salt and pepper.
9. Dip each piece in flour, shake off any excess, followed by egg and then the seasoned breadcrumbs.
10. Place the fish pieces onto a slotted Vortex Oven baking tray, allowing room in between each piece for proper air circulation.
11. Once the chips have finished their initial 10 minutes, immediately add the fish to the upper half of the oven. Set the Vortex Oven to Air Fry for another 10 min at 202°C. Turn halfway through.
12. While the fish is cooking combine the mayonnaise, capers, gherkins, parsley, lemon zest and lemon juice in a bowl. Mix well.
13. Serve fish and chips fresh out of the oven with a dollop of tartar sauce and a generous squeeze of lemon.

Air-fryer Fish Tacos
Servings: 4

Ingredients:
- 2 cups shredded green cabbage
- ¼ cup coarsely chopped fresh cilantro
- 1 scallion, thinly sliced
- 5 tablespoons lime juice (from 2 limes), divided
- 1 tablespoon avocado oil
- 1 large avocado
- 2 tablespoons sour cream
- 1 small clove garlic, grated
- ¼ teaspoon salt
- 1 large egg white
- ⅓ cup dry whole-wheat breadcrumbs
- 1 tablespoon chili powder
- 1 pound skinless mahi-mahi fillets, cut into 2- to 3-inch strips
- Avocado oil cooking spray
- 8 (6 inch) corn tortillas, warmed
- 1 medium tomato, chopped

Directions:
1. Toss cabbage, cilantro, scallion, 2 tablespoons lime juice and avocado oil together in a medium bowl; set aside.
2. Cut avocado in half lengthwise; using a spoon, scoop the pulp into the bowl of a mini food processor. Add sour cream, garlic, salt and the remaining 3 tablespoons lime juice; process until smooth, about 30 seconds. (Alternatively, mash with a fork to reach desired consistency.) Set aside.
3. Preheat air fryer to 400°F. Place egg white in a shallow dish; whisk until frothy. Combine breadcrumbs and chili powder in a separate shallow dish. Pat fish dry with a

paper towel. Coat the fish with egg white, letting excess drip off; dredge in the breadcrumb mixture, pressing to adhere.
4. Working in batches if needed, arrange the fish in an even layer in the fryer basket; coat the fish well with cooking spray. Cook until crispy and golden on one side, about 3 minutes. Flip the fish; coat with cooking spray and cook until it's crispy and flakes easily, about 3 minutes. Flake the fish into bite-size pieces. Top each tortilla evenly with fish, avocado crema (about 1 tablespoon each), cabbage slaw (about 1/4 cup each) and tomato. Serve with lime wedges, if desired.

Air Fryer Tilapia

Servings: 3-4
Cooking Time: 10 Minutes

Ingredients:
- 4 tilapia fillets
- 2 tablespoons olive oil
- 1/2 teaspoon paprika
- 1/2 teaspoon garlic powder
- 1/2 teaspoon onion powder
- 1/2 teaspoon salt
- 1/2 teaspoon black pepper
- FOR SERVING (OPTIONAL)
- Lemon wedges

Directions:
1. Preheat your air fryer to 400 degrees.
2. Place the tilapia fillets on a large plate and drizzle with olive oil.
3. In a small bowl, mix the paprika, garlic powder, onion powder, salt, and pepper.
4. Sprinkle seasoning evenly over the fillets then place in a single layer in the air fryer.
5. Cook tilapia for 10 minutes, flipping the fillets halfway through cooking.
6. Remove the tilapia from the air fryer, serve with lemon wedges (if desired), and enjoy!

NOTES
HOW TO REHEAT TILAPIA IN THE AIR FRYER:
Preheat your air fryer to 400 degrees.
Place leftover tilapia in the air fryer and cook for about 4 minutes, until heated through.
Remove them from the air fryer and enjoy!
HOW TO COOK FROZEN TILAPIA IN THE AIR FRYER:
Preheat your air fryer to 400 degrees.
Spray basket with cooking oil, place the frozen tilapia in the air fryer, and cook for about 13 minutes, until heated through, then enjoy!

Air Fryer Lobster Tail

Servings: 4
Cooking Time: 5 Minutes

Ingredients:
- 4 5-oz Lobster tails
- 1/4 cup Salted butter (melted; 1/2 stick)
- 2 cloves Garlic (crushed)
- 2 tsp Lemon juice
- 1/2 tsp Smoked paprika
- 1 pinch Cayenne pepper (or more if you want extra heat)

Directions:
1. If tails are frozen, thaw them overnight in the fridge, or in a bag submerged in cold water on the counter for about 30 minutes.
2. Preheat the air fryer to 400 degrees F (204 degrees C) for a few minutes.
3. Butterfly the lobster tails. Using kitchen shears, cut down the center of the shell lengthwise, starting from the end opposite the tail fins, continuing down until you reach the tail but without cutting the tail. You want to cut through the top of the shell, but don't cut through the bottom shell. Use your thumbs and fingers to spread open the shell on top, then use your thumbs and fingers to spread open the shell. Run a bamboo skewer through the center of the flesh lengthwise to prevent curling.
4. In a small bowl, whisk together the melted butter, garlic, lemon juice, smoked paprika, and cayenne. Brush the butter mixture over the lobster meat.
5. Cook lobster tails in the air fryer for 5-6 minutes for 5-ounce lobster tails, or until

the meat is opaque and internal temperature in the thickest part reaches 140 degrees F (60 degrees C). (If your tails are a different size, a good rule of thumb for lobster tail air fryer time is about 1 minute per ounce of individual tail. For example, if your lobster tails are 8 ounces each, you'll air fry them for about 8 minutes.) After cooking for 1 minute per ounce of individual tail, check the internal temperature with a meat thermometer and if they are not done yet, cook for 1-3 more minutes as needed.

Air Fryer Crispy Fish Fillets

Servings: 3
Cooking Time: 15 Minutes

Ingredients:
- 1 pound (454 g) white fish fillets (cod, halibut, tilapia, etc.)
- 1 teaspoon (5 ml) kosher salt, or to taste
- 1/2 teaspoon (2.5 ml) black pepper, or to taste
- 1 teaspoon (5 ml) garlic powder
- 1 teaspoon (5 ml) paprika
- 1-2 cups (60-120 g) breading of choice breadcrumbs, panko, crushed pork rinds or almond flour
- 1 egg, or more if needed
- Cooking Spray
- EQUIPMENT
- Air Fryer
- Air Fryer Parchment Paper (optional)
- Perforated Silicone Mats (optional)

Directions:
1. Preheat the Air Fryer at 380°F/193°C for 4 minutes.
2. If using frozen filets, make sure to thaw first. Cut fish filets in half if needed. Make sure they are even sized so they'll cook evenly. The thicker they are, the longer they will take to cook. Pat the filets dry. Lightly oil the filets and then season with the salt, black pepper, garlic powder, and paprika.
3. Put the breading in a shallow bowl. In another bowl, beat the eggs. Dip the filets in the egg, shaking off excess egg. Dredge the filets in your breading of choice. Press filets into the bowl of breading so that they completely coat the filets. Repeat this process for all fish pieces.
4. Line air fryer basket or tray with perforated parchment paper or perforated silicone mat (highly recommended - if you don't have perforated parchment paper or mat, make sure to generously coat the air fryer basket with oil spray). Lightly spray parchment paper with oil spray. Lay coated fish in a single layer on the parchment (cook in batches if needed). Generously spray all sides of the breaded filets with oil spray to coat any dry spots.
5. Air Fry at 380°F/193°C for 8-14 minutes, depending on the size and thickness of your filets. After 6 minutes, flip the filets. Lightly spray any dry spots than then continue cooking for the remaining time or until they are crispy brown and the fish is cooked through. Serve with your favorite dip: tartar sauce, mustard, aioli, etc.

Air Fryer Salmon And Swiss Chard

Servings: 4

Ingredients:
- 1 medium red onion (sliced 1/2 inch thick)
- 1 1/2 tbsp. oil, divided
- Kosher salt and pepper
- 1 large bunch red Swiss chard (thick stems discarded, leaves chopped)
- 2 cloves garlic (sliced)
- 4 5-oz. salmon fillets
- Chili oil, for serving

Directions:
1. Heat air fryer to 385°F. Toss onion with 1/2 tablespoon oil and a pinch each of salt and pepper and air-fry 5 minutes.
2. Toss with Swiss chard, garlic, 1 tablespoon oil, and 1/4 teaspoon each salt and pepper and air-fry until chard and onion are just

tender, about 5 minutes more. Transfer to plates.
3. Season salmon with 1/2 teaspoon each salt and pepper and air-fry at 400°F until skin is crispy and salmon is opaque throughout, 8 to 10 minutes. Serve with chard and drizzle with chili oil if desired.

Air Fryer Shrimp Skewers

Servings: 4
Cooking Time: 9 Minutes

Ingredients:
- 20 large shrimp fresh, peeled

Directions:
1. Soak the wooden skewers in water for 20 minutes.
2. Rinse the shrimp and pat them dry with a paper towel.
3. Place the shrimp on the wooden skewers and then add them in a single layer in the air fryer basket.
4. Air fry the shrimp at 380 degrees Fahrenheit for 8-9 minutes.
5. Carefully remove the shrimp from the air fryer and serve.

NOTES
Serve shrimp skewers over rice, roasted vegetables, or by themselves with cocktail sauce. You can also serve these air fried shrimp over a salad or for shrimp tacos.
You can season the shrimp however you desire. Add a little lemon pepper seasoning, or Old Bay seasoning before cooking. You can also just opt for a little salt and pepper. It's up to you and how you would like to serve them.

Air Fryer Shrimp Fajitas

Servings: 4
Cooking Time: 8 Minutes

Ingredients:
- 1 lb shrimp fresh shrimp, peeled, tails off, deveined
- 1 medium red bell pepper
- 1 medium orange bell pepper
- 1 medium green bell pepper
- 1 medium yellow onion medium
- 2 tbsp fajita seasoning mix
- Toppings:
- 1 small avocado sliced
- 1 teaspoon cilantro fresh, chopped

Directions:
1. Cut the onion and bell peppers into strips and place them in a medium bowl.
2. Rinse the shrimp under water in a colander and then place on a paper towel to pat dry. Add to the bowl with the shrimp.
3. Add the fajita seasoning to the shrimp and bell peppers and toss to coat them evenly.
4. Add the shrimp, peppers, and onion to the basket of the air fryer.
5. Air fry the shrimp and vegetables at 400 degrees Fahrenheit for 8 minutes, tossing the mixture halfway through the cooking process.
6. Carefully remove from the air fryer and serve on a flour tortilla and top with your favorite toppings.

NOTES
This easy air fryer shrimp recipe can be served any way that you want. You can add the ingredients to a large bowl and top it with sour cream, cayenne pepper, and more. It's simple to turn this dish into air fryer shrimp fajita bowls. You can also get flour tortillas or corn tortillas and fill them fully! Perfect for busy weeknights. The best way to serve this recipe is to let everyone add their own toppings and enjoy.

Air Fryer Oven Cheesy Scalloped Potatoes

Ingredients:
- 3 tablespoons butter
- 1 small white or yellow onion, peeled and thinly sliced
- 4 large garlic cloves, minced
- 1/4 cup all-purpose flour
- 1 cup chicken stock or vegetable stock

- 2 cups milk (2% or whole milk, recommended)
- 1 1/2 teaspoons Kosher salt
- 1/2 teaspoon black pepper
- 2 teaspoons fresh thyme leaves, divided
- 10 Yukon Gold Potatoes, sliced into 1/8-inch rounds
- 2 cups freshly-grated sharp cheddar cheese*, divided
- 1/2 cup freshly-grated Parmesan cheese, plus extra for serving

Directions:
1. Prep oven and baking dish: Pre-heat air fryer to 400°F. Grease a 8 x 8-inch baking dish with cooking spray, and set it aside.
2. Sauté the onion and garlic. Melt butter in a large sauté pan over medium-high heat. Add onion, and sauté for 4-5 minutes until soft and translucent. Add garlic and sauté for an additional 1-2 minutes until fragrant. Stir in the flour until it is evenly combined, and cook for 1 more minute.
3. Simmer the sauce. Gradually pour in the stock, and whisk until combined. Add in the milk, salt, pepper, and 1 teaspoon thyme, and whisk until combined. Continue cooking for an additional 1-2 minutes until the sauce just barely begins to simmer around the edges of the pan and thickens. Then remove from heat and set aside.
4. Layer the potatoes. Spread half of the sliced potatoes in an even layer on the bottom of the pan. Top evenly with half of the cream sauce. Then sprinkle evenly with 1 cup of the shredded cheddar cheese, and all of the Parmesan cheese. Top evenly with the remaining sliced potatoes, the other half of the cream sauce, and the remaining 1 cup of cheddar cheese.
5. Bake: Cover the pan with aluminum foil and bake at 400 degrees for 40 minutes. The sauce should be nice and bubbly around the edges. Then remove the foil and bake uncovered for 10-15 minutes, or until the potatoes are cooked through.
6. Cool. Transfer the pan to a cooling rack, and sprinkle with the remaining teaspoon of thyme and extra Parmesan.
7. Serve. Serve warm.

Air-fried Beer Battered Fish Tacos With Mango Salsa Recipe

Ingredients:
- For the fish:
- 2 eggs
- 10 ounces of Mexican beer
- 1 1/2 cups of corn starch
- 1 1/2 cups of flour
- 1/2 tablespoon of chili powder
- 1 tablespoon of cumin
- Kosher salt and fresh cracked pepper to taste
- 1 pound of cod cut into large pieces
- Non-stick spray
- For the Salsa & to make the Taco:
- 3 peeled and medium-diced mangos
- 1/2 peeled, seeded and small diced red bell pepper
- 1 peeled, seeded and small diced jalapeno
- 1/2 peeled and small diced red onion
- 1 tablespoon of chopped fresh cilantro
- Juice of 1 lime
- Kosher salt and fresh cracked pepper to taste
- 1/2 thinly sliced head of red cabbage
- Soft corn tortillas
- Crumbled queso fresco for garnish
- Sliced green onions and cilantro leaves for garnish

Directions:
1. For the salsa:
2. Combine the mangos, peppers, onion, chopped cilantro, lime juice together in a medium size bowl and mix. Refrigerate until ready to serve.
3. For the fish:
4. In a medium size bowl whisk together the eggs and beer and set aside.

5. In a separate medium bowl whisk together the cornstarch, flour, chili powder, cumin, salt and pepper.
6. Coat the fish in the egg-beer mixture and transfer it to the flour mixture and dredge to completely coat on all sides.
7. Spray the bottom of the air fryer basket with no-stick spray and place in the fish and spray the tops of the fish with no-stick spray.
8. Cook at 375 degrees for 15 minutes
9. Place the air fried fish on a corn tortilla and top off with cabbage, salsa, queso fresco, green onions, and cilantro.
10. Enjoy!

Air Fryer Salmon

Servings: 4
Cooking Time: 10 Minutes

Ingredients:
- Salmon Seasoning
- 1 tablespoon paprika
- 1.5 tablespoons garlic powder
- 1 tablespoon brown sugar
- 2 teaspoons kosher salt
- 1 tablespoon dried thyme
- 1 teaspoon mustard powder
- 1 teaspoon black pepper
- Air Fryer Salmon
- 1.5 lbs. salmon filet sliced into 4 salmon steaks
- 1 tablespoon salmon seasoning
- 1 tablespoon olive oil

Directions:
1. First, combine all of the ingredients for the salmon seasoning. Mix to combine. Set aside. Note that you will have leftover salmon seasoning, so make sure to transfer the leftovers into a jar for later.
2. Preheat the air fryer to 400°F. Spray the air fryer basket with non-stick cooking spray.
3. Pat the salmon steaks with a paper towel to remove moisture and then sprinkle steaks with 1 tablespoon of salmon seasoning. Be sure each steak is coated in seasoning (don't worry about getting any of the seasoning on the skin).
4. Place the salmon skin-side down in the air fryer. Drizzle the salmon with the remaining olive oil. Be sure the salmon steaks are not overcrowded or touching (two batches may be needed depending on the size of the air fryer).
5. Cook the salmon for 7-8 minutes at 400°F.
6. Use a fork to test to see if the salmon is done. If that salmon flakes apart easily, remove it from the air fryer. If the salmon is not done, cook it for 1-minute increments until it is done cooking.
7. Let the salmon rest for 5 minutes and enjoy.

Tips & Notes
Want to cook from frozen? Place frozen salmon portions skin-side down onto your air fryer basket. Cook at 400°F for 7-9 minutes to defrost. Then, follow the recipe as directed.
The salmon seasoning becomes a delicious thin crust on the outside of the salmon. It creates a blackened look so don't be worried if it looks burnt.

Air Fryer Keto Coconut Shrimp

Servings: 8
Cooking Time: 10 Minutes

Ingredients:
- 25 large shrimp peeled and deveined
- 1/2 cup coconut flour
- 1 3/4 cup coconut flakes unsweetened
- 3 eggs
- 1 tbsp ground black pepper
- 1 tsp smoked paprika
- 1 tsp salt

Directions:
1. Preheat the Air Fryer to 390 degrees Fahrenheit. Prepare the air fryer basket with non stick cooking spray.
2. Arrange three bowls. Add the coconut flour, paprika, salt and pepper to one bowl. Coconut flakes to the second bowl, and beaten eggs in the third bowl.

3. Dip the shrimp into the coconut flour mixture, then dip into the egg mixture, and finally into the coconut flakes. Set aside on a wire rack until you've finished with all of the shrimp.
4. Add the coconut shrimp in a single layer into the prepared air fryer basket and cook for 8-10 minutes at 380 degrees Fahrenheit. Flip the shrimp halfway through.
5. Remove when golden brown and serve immediately.

NOTES

If you have any "hanging" coconut flakes they will likely brown faster than the shrimp. Air fryers also cook differently and have different wattages. You may need to add or take away time for this recipe depending on the type of air fryer you own.

Air-fryer Salmon With Teriyaki Glaze

Servings: 4
Cooking Time: 10 Minutes

Ingredients:
- 460g skinless salmon fillets
- 1/4 cup teriyaki sauce
- 450g microwave long-grain white rice
- 350g Asian-style salad kit
- 3 tsp sesame seeds, toasted
- 2 spring onions, thinly sliced

Directions:
1. Preheat air fryer to 200°C for 3 minutes. Place salmon in a shallow dish. Pour over sauce and turn to coat. Line air fryer basket with baking paper, trimming to fit. Using tongs, place salmon in paper-lined basket. Slide pan and basket into appliance. Set timer for 8 minutes. Cook, basting with any remaining sauce halfway through cooking time, or until cooked to your liking.
2. Meanwhile, heat rice according to packet instructions. Prepare salad according to kit instructions.
3. Transfer rice to a bowl. Stir in two-thirds of the sesame seeds. Divide rice mixture and salad among bowls. Top with salmon and any cooking juices. Serve scattered with onion and remaining sesame seeds.

Air Fryer Frozen Fish Sticks

Cooking Time: 10 Minutes

Ingredients:
- 1 package frozen fish sticks
- tartar sauce for dipping

Directions:
1. Preheat the air fryer to 400°F.
2. Place the fish sticks in a single layer in the air fryer basket.
3. Cook for 9 10 minutes flipping the sticks halfway through cooking.
4. Serve with tartar sauce.

Air Fryer Calamari

Servings: 4
Cooking Time: 10 Minutes

Ingredients:
- 1/2 cup All purpose flour
- 1 large egg
- 1/3 cup milk regular
- 2 cups panko breadcrumbs
- 1 teaspoon sea salt
- 1 teaspoon ground black pepper
- 1/2 teaspoon paprika
- 1/2 teaspoon garlic powder
- 1 pound calamari rings fresh or frozen
- 1 teaspoon olive oil cooking spray

Directions:
1. Preheat air fryer to 400 degrees F.
2. Create a dredging station with the egg and milk, flour mixture and seasoned breadcrumbs.
3. Place flour in a shallow dish. Set flour aside.
4. In a separate shallow dish whisk the egg and milk together. Set milk mixture aside.
5. In a third separate bowl combine panko, salt, pepper, paprika, and garlic powder together. Set breadcrumb mixture aside.
6. Rinse the calamari with cold water.

7. Then pat the calamari rings dry with a paper towel before dipping to remove excess water.
8. Dip calamari rings in flour (shake off excess flour), then into the egg mixture, and finally in the seasoned panko mixture.
9. Place the calamari rings in a single layer into the air fryer basket. Place extra rings on a baking sheet if working in batches.
10. Spray tops of rings with nonstick cooking spray.
11. Air fry at 400 degrees F for 4 minutes. Flip rings at this point in the cooking process then spray tops with olive oil cooking spray. Continue to air fry for an additional 2-3 minutes or until golden brown and have crispy calamari.
12. If using frozen calamari rings, you may need to add 2-4 minutes of additional cook time. Do not overcook or you will get tough calamari.
13. Place calamari on a wire rack so they remain crispy. Add a sprinkle of salt and black pepper as soon as they are removed from the air fryer.

NOTES
Optional Favorite Dipping Sauce: Cocktail sauce, marinara sauce, tartar sauce, sweet chili sauce, hot sauce, garlic aioli, bechamel sauce or homemade lemon garlic aioli.
Optional Additional Toppings: Lemon wedges, chopped parsley, grated parmesan cheese or fresh lemon juice.Kitchen Tips: You will find fresh or frozen calamari in most local grocery stores.
Substitutions: Use parchment paper for easier clean up. Avocado oil spray instead of olive oil. Use cassava flour or tapioca flour instead of all-purpose flour. Swap out milk for one cup buttermilk.

Air Fryer Coconut Shrimp
Servings: 4
Ingredients:
- FOR THE SHRIMP
- 1/2 c. all-purpose flour
- Kosher salt
- Freshly ground black pepper
- 1 c. panko bread crumbs
- 1/2 c. shredded sweetened coconut
- 2 large eggs, beaten
- 1 lb. large tail-on shrimp, peeled and deveined
- 1/2 c. mayonnaise
- 1 tbsp. sriracha
- 1 tbsp. Thai sweet chili sauce

Directions:
1. In a shallow bowl, season flour with salt and black pepper. In another shallow bowl, combine panko and coconut. In a third shallow bowl, beat eggs to blend.
2. Working one at a time, dip shrimp into seasoned flour, shaking off any excess. Dip into eggs, then into panko mixture, gently pressing to adhere.
3. Working in batches if necessary, in an air-fryer basket, arrange shrimp in a single layer. Cook at 400° until shrimp is golden brown and cooked through, 7 to 9 minutes.
4. In a small bowl, combine mayonnaise, sriracha, and chili sauce.
5. Arrange shrimp on a platter. Serve with dipping sauce alongside.

Crisp-skinned Air Fryer Salmon With Salsa Verde
Servings: 4
Cooking Time: 25 Minutes
Ingredients:
- 4 x 185g salmon fillets, skin on
- 1 tablespoon extra virgin olive oil
- 2 teaspoon sea salt flakes
- 1 small shallot, chopped finely
- 1 clove garlic, crushed
- 2 teaspoon finely grated lemon rind
- 2 tablespoon lemon juice

- 2 tablespoon finely chopped dill
- ¼ cup chopped flat-leaf parsley
- 2 tablespoon chopped chives
- 1 tablespoon baby capers, chopped coarsely
- to serve: extra sea salt flakes

Directions:
1. Preheat a 7-litre air fryer to 200°C/400°F for 3 minutes.
2. Rub salmon with oil, then sprinkle with salt flakes.
3. Taking care, line the air fryer basket with a silicone mat, if available. Place salmon, skin-side up, in the basket; at 200°C/400°F, cook for 8 minutes until skin is crisp and salmon is cooked to your liking.
4. Meanwhile, to make salsa verde, combine remaining ingredients in a medium bowl; mix well. Season.
5. Serve salmon topped with salsa verde and sprinkled with extra salt flakes.

Air Fryer Bacon Wrapped Scallops

Servings: 4
Cooking Time: 13 Minutes

Ingredients:
- 16 large sea scallops cleaned & pat dry with paper towels
- 8 slices center cut bacon
- 1/4 cup Williamson Bros. BBQ sauce

Directions:
1. Slice bacon in half and place the bacon in the air fryer to partially cook at 400 for 3 minutes.
2. 16 large sea scallops
3. Pat the scallops dry with paper towels to remove any moisture.
4. Wrap each scallop in 1/2 slice of bacon and secure it with a toothpick.
5. 8 slices center cut bacon
6. Place scallops in air fryer (I can fit 8 at a time in my basket style air fryer)
7. Lightly brush scallop with your favorite barbecue sauce. I recommend a thinner sauce – not a heavy thick sauce. You can also just spray with olive oil and salt/pepper.
8. Cook at 400 for 5 minutes. Turn scallops delicately and baste again with bbq sauce. Cook for another 5 minutes at 400 until scallop is tender and opaque and bacon is cooked through. Serve hot.
9. 1/4 cup Williamson Bros. BBQ sauce
10. I also sprinkled a little Historic BBQ Red seasoning on them when they were done.

Air Fryer Honey Mustard Salmon Recipe

Servings: 3
Cooking Time: 10 Minutes

Ingredients:
- 3 salmon fillets 1 ½ inches thick
- salt and pepper
- 2 tablespoons honey
- 1 tablespoon Dijon mustard

Directions:
1. Make a foil sling for the air fryer basket, about 4 inches tall and a few inches longer than the width of the basket. Lay foil widthwise across basket, pressing it into and up the sides. Lightly spray foil and basket with cooking spray.
2. Pat salmon dry with paper towels. Season with salt and pepper.
3. In a small bowl, mix together honey and Dijon, until well combined. Reserve 1 tablespoon of glaze. Drizzle remaining glaze evenly over salmon fillets, tops and sides.
4. Arrange fillets skin side down on sling in the basket, with space between them. (The number of fillets you can fit in your air fryer at one time depends on the size of the fillets and the size of your air fryer.)
5. Cook at 350°F/175°C for 8-10 minutes, until salmon flakes easily and registers at 145°F/62.8°C (thinner salmon will be ready sooner, thicker salmon will take more time).

6. Using sling, carefully lift salmon from air fryer. Loosen the skin with a fish spatula or utensil, then transfer fillets to plate, leaving skin behind.
7. Drizzle reserved sauce over fillets. Garnish with fresh parsley, if desired. Serve warm.

Cajun Air Fryer Fish
Ingredients:
- Fresh fish fillets. Use any sustainable white fish. I used hake but halibut, cod, tilapia, bass, grouper, haddock, snapper or catfish will all work well.
- Olive oil - Vegetable oil like avocado oil is a good substitution
- Cajun seasoning/Cajun spice. Most supermarkets will have a cajun spice blend in their spice aisle.
- Smoked paprika
- Garlic powder. Onion powder can also be used
- Fresh lemon juice

Directions:
1. Slice the fish into portions then place in the air fryer basket. In a small bowl, mix the olive oil, lemon juice and seasonings together then spoon over the fish. I don't usually add parchment paper to the basket but you can if you're worried about the fish sticking. You can also spray the basket with cooking spray or olive oil. Air fry for 8-10 minutes at 200°C/400°F until the fish is caramelized on the outside and opaque and juicy on the inside. Cooking time will depend on the thickness of the fish but generally fish is cooked when it flakes apart easily and a fork can be inserted without any resistance. Remove from the air fryer then serve with lemon wedges.

Haddock Croquettes
Servings: 4
Ingredients:
- 75g fresh breadcrumbs
- 2 tsp Sherry
- 500g uncooked haddock fillets, flaked
- 3 eggs
- 1 bunch fresh parsley, finely chopped
- 1 ½ tsp dried coriander
- ½ tsp salt
- ¼ tsp white pepper
- Zest of 1 lemon
- 100g plain flour
- 150g dried breadcrumbs
- Rapeseed oil for spraying
- COOKING MODE
- When entering cooking mode - We will enable your screen to stay 'always on' to avoid any unnecessary interruptions whilst you cook!

Directions:
1. In a bowl, add fresh breadcrumbs, flaked fish fillets and Sherry. Mash well to combine, beat one egg and add in with chopped parsley, coriander, pepper, salt and lemon zest. Mix well.
2. Prepare three shallow dishes for dipping the fish. One dish with flour, one dish with breadcrumbs and one dish with the remaining 2 eggs, beaten well. Line a baking tray with baking parchment.
3. Flour your hands and form croquettes from the mixture that are about 5-7cm in length. Roll the croquettes first in flour, then in egg, and finally in the breadcrumbs and place them on the tray.
4. Insert the crisper plates in zone 1 and 2 drawers. Spray plate with rapeseed oil. Place croquettes on crisper plate and spray croquettes with oil. Select AIR FRY, set temperature to 200°C and set time to 10 minutes. Select MATCH. Press START/STOP to begin.
5. When cook time is finished, use silicone coated tongs to remove the croquettes to a serving dish.
6. Serve immediately with a salad, tartar sauce and lemon.

POULTRY RECIPES

Air Fryer Stir Fry
Servings: 4
Cooking Time: 7 Minutes

Ingredients:
- 1 pound boneless chicken breast or thighs, cut into bite size pieces
- 1 tablespoon sesame oil
- 1/4 cup soy sauce
- 2 tablespoons brown sugar packed
- 1 teaspoon chili powder
- 1 teaspoon freshly grated ginger
- 1/2 cup white onion sliced
- 1 cup portabella mushrooms sliced
- 1 medium red bell pepper sliced
- 1 medium orange or yellow bell pepper sliced
- 1 cup snow peas fresh or frozen

Directions:
1. In a small bowl, combine sesame oil, soy sauce, brown sugar, chili powder, and freshly grated ginger. Whisk together until well combined.
2. Pour sauce into a large shallow dish, or sealable bag. Add in the chicken pieces and toss until the chicken is covered in the sauce. Let meat pieces marinate for at least 30 minutes to an hour in your refrigerator.
3. Lightly spray the air fryer basket with olive oil cooking spray. Then transfer marinated chicken to the air fryer basket. Toss in the mushrooms, onion, bell peppers and snow peas into the basket.
4. Air fry at 380 degrees F for 7-9 minutes, toss food midway through the cooking process, until chicken has finish cooking and has an internal temperature of 165 degrees F.

NOTES
Optional Additional Flavors: Garlic powder, orange sauce, black pepper, dark soy sauce, Italian seasoning, a few cloves garlic, hot sauce, a tablespoon rice vinegar, dry sherry or white vinegar.

Optional Toppings: Sesame seeds, sliced green onion, chopped peanuts, crushed potato chips, lemon wedges or zest, the crispiness of bacon bits or crunchy coating from breadcrumbs.
Substitutions: Frozen vegetables can replace fresh ones (cook time may slightly vary). Use tamari for gluten free option (tastes like soy but does not have wheat in it). Use vegetable oil, grapeseed oil or avocado oil if you do not have sesame oil.

Air Fryer Turkey Bacon
Servings: 4
Cooking Time: 6 Minutes

Ingredients:
- 8 slices turkey bacon (cured or uncured)

Directions:
1. Preheat your air fryer to 400 degrees.
2. Place the turkey bacon in the air fryer and cook for 5 to 6 minutes. Cook uncured bacon that's a little wider for about 8 to 9 minutes. Flip the bacon halfway through cooking.
3. Remove the turkey bacon from the air fryer and enjoy!

NOTES
To make extra crispy turkey bacon slices, add an extra 1 to 2 minutes to the cooking time.

Air Fryer Fried Chicken
Servings: 3

Ingredients:
- 2 lb. skin-on, bone-in chicken pieces (a mix of cuts)
- 2 c. buttermilk
- 1/2 c. hot sauce
- 3 tsp. kosher salt, divided
- 2 c. all-purpose flour
- 1 tsp. garlic powder
- 1 tsp. onion powder
- 1/2 tsp. dried oregano

- 1/2 tsp. freshly ground black pepper
- 1/4 tsp. cayenne pepper

Directions:
1. Trim chicken of any excess fat and transfer to a large bowl. In a medium bowl, combine buttermilk, hot sauce, and 2 teaspoons salt. Pour buttermilk mixture over chicken, making sure all pieces are coated. Cover bowl and refrigerate at least 1 hour or up to overnight.
2. In a shallow bowl or pie dish, combine flour, garlic powder, onion powder, oregano, black pepper, cayenne, and remaining 1 teaspoon salt. Working one at a time, remove chicken from buttermilk mixture, shaking off any excess. Place in flour mixture, turning to coat.
3. Working in batches if necessary, in an air-fryer basket, arrange chicken (do not overcrowd). Cook at 400°, turning halfway through, until chicken is golden brown and an instant-read thermometer inserted into thickest part registers 165°, 20 to 25 minutes.

Air Fryer Southwest Chicken

Servings: 3
Cooking Time: 19 Minutes

Ingredients:
- 3 boneless chicken breasts 7 ounces each
- 2 tablespoons lime juice
- 1 tablespoon olive oil
- ½ teaspoon chili powder
- ½ teaspoon cumin
- ¼ teaspoon garlic powder
- ¼ teaspoon salt

Directions:
1. Preheat air fryer to 370°F.
2. Toss chicken with seasonings, oil, and lime juice.
3. Place chicken breasts in a single layer in the air fryer basket.
4. Cook for 16-19 minutes flipping chicken after 10 minutes.
5. Rest 5 minutes before slicing.

Notes: Ensure chicken reaches an internal temperature of 165°F. Check the chicken early, do not overcook.
These are great sliced and served in taco shells or tortillas.

Air Fryer Chicken Parmesan

Servings: 4
Cooking Time: 35 Minutes

Ingredients:
- 2 boneless, skinless chicken breasts
- 1 cup bread crumbs (regular, panko, or combo)
- ½ cup shredded Parmesan cheese, divided
- 2 teaspoons Italian seasoning
- 1 teaspoon garlic powder
- ½ teaspoon kosher salt
- 2 large eggs
- ½ cup marinara sauce, plus more for serving
- ½ mozzarella cheese, shredded

Directions:
1. Preheat your air fryer to 350 degrees. Cut the chicken breasts in half horizontally, pounding them to even thickness as needed; set aside.
2. In a shallow bowl, combine bread crumbs, all but 2 tablespoons of Parmesan, Italian seasoning, garlic powder, and salt. In a second bowl, whisk the eggs.
3. Dip each piece of chicken in the egg, and let the excess egg drip off. Press the chicken pieces into the breadcrumb mixture, coating evenly.
4. Place the chicken in a single layer in the air fryer. Spray the top of the chicken with cooking spray. (You will likely need to do this in batches.)
5. Air fry for 8-11 minutes, flipping halfway, until the chicken is golden and mostly cooked through. Carefully spread 2 tablespoons of marinara sauce over each breast, then sprinkle with mozzarella. Continue cooking for 2-3 minutes, until the cheese is melted and the chicken is cooked through to 165 degrees F.

Air Fryer Turkey Breast

Servings: 10
Cooking Time: 55 Minutes

Ingredients:
- 4 pound turkey breast (on the bone with skin (ribs removed))
- 1 tablespoon olive oil
- 2 teaspoons kosher
- 1/2 tablespoon dry turkey or poultry seasoning (I used Bell's which has not salt)

Directions:
1. Rub 1/2 tablespoon of oil all over the turkey breast. Season both sides with salt and turkey seasoning then rub in the remaining half tablespoon of oil over the skin side.
2. Preheat the air fryer 350F and cook skin side down 20 minutes, turn over and cook until the internal temperature is 160F using an instant-read thermometer about 30 to 40 minutes more depending on the size of your breast. Let is rest 10 minutes before carving.

Notes
Without the skin the smart points will be 0.

Air Fryer Whole Turkey With Gravy

Servings: 12
Cooking Time: 3 Hrs 15 Minutes

Ingredients:
- 14 lb. (6.35 kg) raw Whole Turkey
- 6 Tablespoons (90 g) butter, cut into slices
- 4 cloves garlic, sliced thin
- 1 Tablespoon (15 ml) kosher salt, or to taste
- black pepper, to taste
- Olive Oil (or oil of choice), to coat turkey
- 1 1/2 cups (360 ml) chicken broth
- 3/4 cup (95 g) all purpose flour (for the gravy)
- EQUIPMENT
- Halogen Air Fryer
- Instant Read Thermometer (optional)

Directions:
1. Thaw your turkey completely on the inside cavity. Remove and giblets and neck bones from the turkey cavity (many times the giblet pack will be tucked under the skin by the neck). Pat the turkey dry.
2. Tuck the butter slices and garlic in-between the skin and the turkey breasts. Rub olive oil over the turkey and season with salt and pepper.
3. Place the lower rack in the air fryer and spray with oil. Place the turkey breast side down in the air fryer. Pour in 1/2 cup of broth over the turkey. Place the extender ring and lid on the air fryer.
4. Air Fry the turkey at 350°F for about 2 1/2 to 3 hours.
5. Every 30 minutes, baste with chicken broth (the first 2 bastes will be with the remaining broth. After that, baste from the broth & juices at the bottom of the air fryer).
6. After cooking for 2 hours, take off the air fryer lid and extender ring. Lift the turkey out, flip to breast side up, and then place back into the air fryer. Baste the turkey and then place the extender ring and lid back on
7. Continue to Air Fry at 350°F until the turkey reaches an internal temperature of 165°F at the thickest parts of the thigh, wings and breast, and the juices run clear when you cut between the leg and the thigh (about 30 minutes - 1 hour).
8. Let rest for about 15-20 minutes.
9. While the turkey rests, make the gravy. Remove the lower rack from the air fryer. Leaving the turkey juices and broth in the air fryer, skim the chunks from the drippings and broth.
10. Place flour in a medium bowl. Ladle in about 1 cup of the drippings and broth into the flour and whisk until smooth. Pour the flour mixture into the air fryer with the remaining drippings and broth. Whisk until smooth.
11. Place the air fryer lid back on and Air Fry at 400°F for 10 minutes or until thickened, whisking a couple times while cooking.

Air-fryer Southern-style Chicken

Servings: 6
Cooking Time: 20 Minutes

Ingredients:
- 2 cups crushed Ritz crackers (about 50)
- 1 tablespoon minced fresh parsley
- 1 teaspoon garlic salt
- 1 teaspoon paprika
- 1/2 teaspoon pepper
- 1/4 teaspoon ground cumin
- 1/4 teaspoon rubbed sage
- 1 large egg, beaten
- 1 broiler/fryer chicken (3 to 4 pounds), cut up
- Cooking spray

Directions:
1. Preheat air fryer to 375°. In a shallow bowl, mix the first 7 ingredients. Place egg in a separate shallow bowl. Dip chicken in egg, then in cracker mixture, patting to help coating adhere. In batches, place chicken in a single layer on greased tray in air-fryer basket; spritz with cooking spray.
2. Cook 10 minutes. Turn chicken and spritz with cooking spray. Cook until chicken is golden brown and juices run clear, 10-20 minutes longer.

Frozen Chicken Thighs In The Air Fryer

Servings: 4-6
Cooking Time: 30 Minutes

Ingredients:
- 1 1/2 to 2 pounds frozen chicken thighs
- 1 tablespoon McCormick Lemon Pepper Seasoning

Directions:
1. Preheat your air fryer to 380 degrees F.
2. Place separated frozen chicken thighs in the air fryer and cook for 15 minutes until the chicken is just thawed.
3. Remove the chicken from the basket.
4. Spray each thigh with cooking oil, then sprinkle on the lemon pepper seasoning evenly.
5. Return the chicken to the basket and cook for 12-15 additional minutes, flipping once halfway through.
6. Remove the chicken thighs from the air fryer and enjoy with your favorite sides.

NOTES
HOW TO REHEAT CHICKEN THIGHS IN THE AIR FRYER
Preheat the air fryer to 350 degrees F.
Place the leftover chicken thighs in the air fryer.
Cook for 3 to 5 minutes until heated through.
How to Cook Thawed Chicken Thighs in the Air Fryer:
Preheat your air fryer to 380 degrees.
Coat the chicken thighs evenly with Lemon Pepper seasoning then place in the air fryer in a single layer.
Cook for 12 to 15 minutes until chicken reaches 165 degrees.

Turkey Stuffed Air-fried Peppers

Servings: 3

Ingredients:
- 3 medium red sweet peppers
- 1 tablespoon olive oil
- 12 ounce ground turkey
- ½ cup cooked brown rice
- ¼ cup panko breadcrumbs
- ¾ cup low-sodium marinara sauce
- 3 tablespoon finely chopped flat-leaf parsley
- ¼ teaspoon ground pepper
- ¼ cup grated Parmesan cheese (1 oz.)
- ¼ cup shredded part-skim mozzarella cheese (1 oz.)

Directions:
1. Coat the basket of an air fryer with cooking spray. Cut tops off peppers and reserve. Seed the peppers and set aside.
2. Heat oil in a large skillet over medium-high heat. Add turkey; cook, stirring occasionally, until browned, about 4 minutes. Stir in rice and panko; cook,

stirring occasionally, until warmed through, about 1 minute. Remove from heat and stir in marinara, parsley, pepper and Parmesan. Divide the mixture evenly among the prepared peppers.

3. Place the peppers in the prepared air-fryer basket. Nestle the pepper tops in the bottom of the basket. Cook at 350°F until the peppers are tender, about 8 minutes. Top with mozzarella; cook until the cheese is melted, about 2 minutes more.

Air Fryer Lebanese Chicken

Servings: 4
Cooking Time: 35 Minutes

Ingredients:
- 1 whole chicken 2-3 lbs cut up into 8 pieces
- 1 tbsp olive oil
- 2 tsp salt
- 1 tsp pepper
- 1 tsp ground coriander
- 1 tsp onion powder
- 1/2 tsp cumin
- 1/4 tsp cinnamon
- 1/2 large yellow onion cut into ½" pieces
- 3 cloves garlic grated
- 1/2 lemon juiced
- fresh chopped parsley garnish

Directions:
1. In a small mixing bowl, combine all of the spices- salt, pepper, coriander, onion powder, cumin, and cinnamon.
2. Place the chicken on a large mixing bowl and toss with olive oil. Then add the spice mixture and toss again to coat the chicken.
3. Add the chicken, onions, garlic, and lemon juice into a large ziplock bag and marinate for at least 30 minutes, up to over night.
4. Once the chicken has finished marinating, remove from the ziplock bag and place in the air fryer basket.
5. Air fry for 35 to 40 minutes at 350 F or until the thickest part of the chicken has reached an internal temperature of 165 F.

Notes

If there is moisture on the chicken, pat them dry with a paper towel before adding the oil and seasoning. Patting dry the chicken helps the seasoning stick much better.

You can easily turn this Lebanese chicken into a wrap or salad. After you air fry the chicken, allow it to rest before shredding the chicken to stuff into a warm naan or pita bread or place it overtop of a salad.

The easiest way to make sure the chicken is ready is by using an instant-read thermometer. The chicken should have an internal temperature of 165F. Be careful not to hit the bone when inserting the thermometer, as it'll lead to an inaccurate read.

If you have time, marinating the chicken overnight makes the chicken even more flavorful.

When placing the Lebanese chicken into the air fryer, place them in a single layer. Avoid stacking them as the chicken will steam instead of crisp up. If your pieces of chicken are on the larger side, you can air fry them in two batches.

Air Fryer Chicken Wings

Servings: 10
Cooking Time: 30 Minutes

Ingredients:
- FOR THE WINGS:
- 1 1/2 pounds chicken wings
- 1 teaspoon kosher salt
- 2 tablespoons unsalted butter
- 1/4 cup hot sauce Frank's RedHot is what I use
- 1 tablespoon minced garlic
- 1/2 tablespoon white vinegar
- Nonstick cooking spray
- TO SERVE:
- Blue cheese sauce The Well Plated Cookbook, page 212 or blue cheese dressing of choice
- Celery sticks
- Chopped fresh chives optional for color

Directions:

1. Coat the basket of a 3 quart or larger air fryer with nonstick spray.
2. Trim off the wing tips (you should be able to feel the joint soft spot). It should separate fairly easily, but if not, put the blade in place, then carefully but firmly hit the top of your knife to apply extra pressure. Discard. Next, split the drumette side of each wing from the flat side at the joint: slice down through the skin feeling for the "soft spot" and wiggle your knife as needed.
3. Pat the wings very dry. Sprinkle all over with salt.
4. Place the wings in the air fryer in a single layer, making sure they do not touch (if needed, stand up the drumettes along the side). Set the air fryer to 360 degrees F. Cook the wings for 12 minutes, then remove the basket and with tongs, flip the wings over. Return to the air fryer at 360 degrees for 12 additional minutes.
5. Slide out the basket, flip the wings once more, then return them to the air fryer. Increase the air fryer temperature to 390 degrees F. Cook the wings for 6 minutes, flipping once more halfway through. The skin should look nice and crisp (if your wings are on the larger side, they may need a few more minutes).
6. While the wings finish up, melt the butter in a large microwave safe bowl in the microwave or a saucepan on the stove. Stir in the hot sauce, garlic, and vinegar until smooth.
7. Transfer the wings to the bowl with the hot sauce mixture. Toss to throughly coat the wings. Transfer the wings to a serving plate. Sprinkle with chives as desired. Enjoy warm with blue cheese sauce and celery.

Notes
TO MAKE IN THE OVEN: Place a broiler rack 4 to 6 inches from the broiler. Preheat to high. Line a rimmed baking sheet with foil and place an oven safe baking rack on top. Arrange the wings on the rack in a single layer so they do not touch. Broil for 20 to 25 minutes, until the wings are browned and crisp, flipping once halfway through.

TO STORE. Refrigerate leftover chicken wings for up to 3 days.

TO REHEAT. Let the wings come to room temperature. Mist with water to help make them juicy, then reheat in the oven at 350 degrees F for 10 to 12 minutes, or the air fryer at 350 degrees F for 6 minutes, turning once halfway through.

Air Fryer Sesame Chicken
Servings: 4
Cooking Time: 24 Minutes

Ingredients:
- Sauce Ingredients:
- 1/4 cup soy sauce
- 2 Tablespoons brown sugar
- 1 teaspoon orange zest
- 5 teaspoons Hoisin sauce
- 1/2 teaspoon ground ginger
- 1 teaspoon minced garlic
- 1 Tablespoon cold water
- 1 Tablespoon corn starch
- 2 teaspoons sesame seeds toasted
- Chicken Ingredients:
- 1 pound chicken thighs boneless skinless
- 1/3 cup corn starch
- 1 teaspoon olive oil spray

Directions:
1. Cut the chicken into cubed chunks, then toss in a large bowl with cornstarch and coat the chicken evenly.
2. Preheat the Air Fryer to 390° Fahrenheit.
3. Add the chicken to the prepared air fryer basket.
4. Air fry the chicken for 24 minutes until golden brown, tossing the chicken halfway through the cooking time. Add a spritz of oil after tossing the chicken.
5. Add the sesame chicken sauce ingredients into a small saucepan and whisk over medium heat until the sauce has reached a small boil.

6. Once the sugar has completely dissolved, whisk in the cornstarch and water. Allow the sauce to thicken for around 5 minutes. Continue to whisk.
7. Mix in the sesame seeds.
8. Remove the sauce from the heat and set aside for 5 minutes, allowing the sauce to continue thickening.
9. Place the chicken into a medium size mixing bowl and cover with the sauce. Toss the chicken so that each piece is coated in sauce.
10. Serve topped over rice and garnish with green onion.

NOTES

Flour is a wonderful substitute for corn starch as it has starch in it already.

However, keep in mind; you will need twice as much flour as cornstarch to make

homemade sesame sauce.

You can also use chicken tenders or chicken breasts instead of chicken thighs.

Instead of corn starch, you can swap out tapioca flour to coat the chicken. You'll still

get crispy chicken without the added carbs.

General Tso's Air-fryer Chicken

Servings: 4

Ingredients:
- 1 large egg
- 1 pound boneless, skinless chicken thighs, patted dry and cut into 1 to 1 1/4-inch chunks
- ⅓ cup plus 2 tsp. cornstarch, divided
- ¼ teaspoon kosher salt
- ¼ teaspoon ground white pepper
- 7 tablespoon lower-sodium chicken broth
- 2 tablespoon lower-sodium soy sauce
- 2 tablespoon ketchup
- 2 teaspoon sugar
- 2 teaspoon unseasoned rice vinegar
- 1 ½ tablespoon canola oil
- 3 - 4 chiles de árbol, chopped and seeds discarded
- 1 tablespoon finely chopped fresh ginger
- 1 tablespoon finely chopped garlic
- 2 tablespoon thinly sliced green onion, divided
- 1 teaspoon toasted sesame oil
- ½ teaspoon toasted sesame seeds

Directions:
1. Beat egg in a large bowl, add chicken, and coat well. In another bowl, combine 1/3 cup cornstarch with salt and pepper. Transfer chicken with a fork to cornstarch mixture, and stir with a spatula to coat every piece.
2. Transfer chicken to air-fryer oven racks (or fryer basket, in batches), leaving a little space between pieces. Preheat air-fryer at 400°F for 3 minutes. Add the battered chicken; cook for 12 to 16 minutes, giving things a shake midway. Let dry 3 to 5 minutes. If chicken is still damp on one side, cook for 1 to 2 minutes more.
3. Whisk together remaining 2 teaspoons cornstarch with broth, soy sauce, ketchup, sugar, and rice vinegar. Heat canola oil and chiles in a large skillet over medium heat. When gently sizzling, add the ginger and garlic; cook until fragrant, about 30 seconds.
4. Re-whisk cornstarch mixture; stir into mixture in skillet. Increase heat to medium-high. When sauce begins to bubble, add chicken. Stir to coat; cook until sauce thickens and nicely clings to chicken, about 1 1/2 minutes. Turn off heat; stir in 1 tablespoon green onion and sesame oil. Transfer to a serving plate, and top with sesame seeds and remaining 1 tablespoon green onion.

Air Fryer Thanksgiving Turkey

Servings: 2-4

Ingredients:
- Deselect All
- 1 teaspoon kosher salt
- 1 teaspoon dried thyme
- 1 teaspoon ground rosemary
- 1/2 teaspoon freshly ground black pepper
- 1/2 teaspoon dried sage

- 1/2 teaspoon garlic powder
- 1/2 teaspoon paprika
- 1/2 teaspoon dark brown sugar
- 1 bone-in, skin-on turkey breast (about 2 1/2 pounds)
- Olive oil, for brushing

Directions:
1. Mix together the salt, thyme, rosemary, pepper, sage, garlic powder, paprika and brown sugar in a small bowl.
2. Brush the turkey breast with olive oil and rub on both sides with the dry rub mixture, making sure to get under the skin wherever possible. Put the turkey skin-side down in the basket of a 3.5-quart air fryer and roast at 360 degrees F for 20 minutes.
3. Carefully open the air fryer and flip the turkey over so it is skin-side up. Close the air fryer and roast until an instant-read thermometer inserted into the thickest part of the meat registers 165 degrees F, about an additional 15 minutes. Let rest at least 10 minutes, then slice and serve.

Air Fryer Whole Chicken
Servings: 6
Cooking Time: 44 Minutes

Ingredients:
- 3 lb whole chicken
- 2 tablespoons olive oil
- 1/2 teaspoon salt
- 1/2 teaspoon pepper
- 1 teaspoon smoked paprika
- 1 teaspoon Italian seasonings
- 1/4 teaspoon Rosemary
- 1/4 teaspoon mustard powder

Directions:
1. Preheat the air fryer to 180C/350F.
2. Pat dry the chicken, then drizzle the olive oil on all sides.
3. In a small bowl, combine all the spices. Rub the spices all over the chicken.
4. Place the chicken in the air fryer breast side down. Air fry for 25 minutes before flipping and cooking for a further 20 minutes. Once the chicken reaches an internal temperature of 165F, remove it from the air fryer.
5. Let the chicken rest for 5 minutes before carving.

Notes
TO STORE: Place leftover chicken in an airtight container and store it in the refrigerator for up to 5 days.
TO FREEZE: Once the chicken has cooled to room temperature, place in a ziplock bag and store it in the freezer for up to 3 months. You can also shred it before doing so.
TO REHEAT: Microwave portions of the chicken for 20-30 seconds or reheat in a preheated oven until warm.

Air Fryer Boneless Chicken Thighs
Servings: 4
Cooking Time: 15 Minutes

Ingredients:
- 4 boneless chicken thighs
- 2 Tablespoons canola oil
- 1 teaspoon brown sugar
- ½ teaspoon paprika
- ½ teaspoon dried parsley
- ½ teaspoon garlic powder
- ½ teaspoon onion powder
- ½ teaspoon salt
- ¼ teaspoon black ground pepper

Directions:
1. Preheat air fryer to 400 degrees F.
2. Pat chicken dry with paper towel then drizzle with oil and toss to coat.
3. Combine brown sugar and seasonings in a small bowl. Rub over chicken thighs.
4. Coat basket with non-aerosol cooking spray then place thighs in air fryer basket and cook for 12-14 minutes, flipping half way if desired, until an internal temperature of 165 degrees F is reached.

Air Fryer Popcorn Chicken With Jalapeño Ranch

Servings: 6
Cooking Time: 15 Minutes

Ingredients:
- 500 g (1lb) chicken breasts
- 1 cup flour
- 2 eggs beaten
- 2 cups panko breadcrumbs
- 1 tsp salt
- 1 tsp smoked paprika
- 1 tsp garlic powder
- 1 tsp dried oregano
- 1 tsp pepper
- For the Jalapeño Ranch
- ½ cup sour cream
- ½ cup mayonnaise
- 1 tbsp Jalapeños chopped
- 2 tsp dill finely chopped
- 1 tsp parsley finely chopped
- 2 tsp chives finely chopped
- 1-2 tsp lime juice
- salt and pepper to taste

Directions:
1. Slice the chicken into bite size chunks.
2. Place the flour, eggs and panko breadcrumbs in separate shallow bowls. Season the flour with salt and pepper. Season the breadcrumbs with the spices.
3. Coat the chicken in the flour, then in the beaten egg and finally in the breadcrumbs mixture. For a thicker coating, repeat the egg and breadcrumb steps.
4. Place the chicken pieces in a single layer in the basket of an air fryer then drizzle or spray with olive oil.
5. Cook the chicken at 200°C/390°F for 15 minutes, turning half way through.
6. Finely chop the herbs and place in a bowl. Mix in the mayonnaise, sour cream, lime juice, jalapeños, salt and pepper. Taste and adjust seasoning if necessary.
7. Remove the popcorn chicken from the air fryer then serve with the ranch and lime wedges.

Air Fryer Cornish Hens

Servings: 2
Cooking Time: 40 Minutes

Ingredients:
- 2 Cornish game hens (about 1.5 lbs./680g each)
- 1 teaspoon (5 ml) garlic powder
- 1 teaspoon (5 ml) smoked paprika
- 1 teaspoon (5 ml) dried basil (or herbs of choice)
- 1 teaspoon (5 ml) salt
- 1 teaspoon (5 ml) black pepper
- oil spray
- EQUIPMENT
- Air Fryer
- Instant Read Thermometer (optional)
- Oil Sprayer (optional)

Directions:
1. In a bowl, combine seasonings (garlic powder, smoked paprika, basil, salt, and pepper).
2. Spray Cornish hens with oil to coat. Rub seasoning mix around the hens.
3. Spray basket/tray of air fryer with oil spray or line with a perforated silicone liner or perforated parchment paper. Lay hens breast side down in the basket/tray.
4. Air Fry at 360°F/182°C for 20 minutes then flip the hens.
5. If needed, crumple some foil and place under the front of the Cornish hens to level them and keep the legs from sticking upwards toward the top of the air fryer where the heating element can get too hot. This will keep the legs from burning.
6. Air Fry for another 12-18 or until internal temperature reaches 165°F/74°C.
7. Allow the hens to rest for 10 minutes before serving.

Air Fryer Tandoori Turkey Breast

Servings: 4

Ingredients:
- 1 split skin-on, bone-in turkey breast (about 1 3/4 lb.)
- 1 1/2 tsp. kosher salt, divided
- 1 c. full-fat plain Greek yogurt
- 2 cloves garlic, minced
- 1 tbsp. sweet paprika
- 2 tsp. ground turmeric
- 2 tsp. minced fresh ginger (from a 1" piece)
- 1 tsp. ground cumin
- Olive oil cooking spray

Directions:
1. Pat turkey dry with paper towels; season all over with 1 teaspoon salt.
2. In a medium bowl, combine yogurt, garlic, paprika, turmeric, ginger, cumin, and remaining 1/2 teaspoon salt. Spread yogurt mixture all over turkey. Let stand at room temperature for 30 minutes.
3. Lightly coat an air-fryer basket with cooking spray. Place turkey in basket. Cook at 350°, flipping every 10 minutes, until turkey is golden brown and an instant-read thermometer inserted into thickest part of breast registers 165°, 35 to 40 minutes. Let turkey rest about 10 minutes before slicing.

Air Fryer Frozen Chicken Strips

Servings: 4
Cooking Time: 14 Minutes

Ingredients:
- 12 ounces (170 g) Frozen Chicken Strips (Tenders) (about 4 strips)
- optional dipping sauce (ketchup, bbq sauce, mustard, hot sauce, ranch, etc.)
- EQUIPMENT
- Air Fryer

Directions:
1. Place the frozen chicken strips in the air fryer basket and spread out into a single even layer. No oil spray is needed.
2. Air Fry at 400°F/205°C for 10 minutes. Flip the chicken over.
3. Continue to cook at 400°F/205°C for another 2-5 minutes or until cooked through and crispy.
4. Serve with your favorite dipping sauce if desired.

NOTES
Air Frying Tips and Notes:
No Oil Necessary. Cook Frozen - Do not thaw first.
Shake or turn if needed. Don't overcrowd the air fryer basket.
Recipe timing is based on a non-preheated air fryer. If cooking in multiple batches of chicken strips back to back, the following batches may cook a little quicker.
Recipes were tested in 3.7 to 6 qt. air fryers. If using a larger air fryer, the chicken might cook quicker so adjust cooking time.
Remember to set a timer to shake/flip/toss as directed in recipe.

Air Fryer Chicken Bites With Parmesan Cheese

Servings: 4
Cooking Time: 18 Minutes

Ingredients:
- 2 teaspoons olive oil
- 2 teaspoons Worcestershire sauce
- 1 teaspoon dried Italian seasoning
- ½ teaspoon garlic powder
- ¼ teaspoon salt
- ⅛ teaspoon freshly ground black pepper
- 1 pound skinless, boneless chicken breast, cut into 1-inch cubes
- 2 tablespoons all-purpose flour
- cooking spray
- ¼ cup shredded Parmesan cheese
- 2 tablespoons chopped fresh parsley

Directions:
1. Whisk olive oil, Worcestershire, Italian seasoning, garlic powder, salt, and pepper together in a bowl. Add chicken cubes and stir to coat.

2. Preheat an air fryer to 370 degrees F (185 degrees C) for 10 minutes.
3. Add flour to the chicken mixture and stir to coat until all liquid is absorbed.
4. Place chicken in the basket of the air fryer and cook for 8 minutes. Using tongs, flip the pieces over. Spray tops with non-stick cooking spray and cook 8 minutes more.
5. Sprinkle Parmesan cheese and parsley over the chicken. Cook until cheese has started to melt, about 2 minutes more. Serve immediately.

Air Fryer 'kfc' Fried Chicken
Ingredients:
- Chicken:
- 8 pieces of free-range chicken – thighs and drumsticks (bone and skin on)
- 250ml buttermilk
- 1 free-range egg
- 1 Tbsp hot sauce (I use Cholula chipotle hot sauce)
- Flour coating:
- 2 cups flour
- 2 tsp salt
- 6 tsp dried herbs (thyme, sage, parsley, oregano, basil)
- 1 Tbsp celery salt
- 1 Tbsp fine white pepper powder (or a mix. Of black and white)
- 2 tsp Hot English mustard powder
- 1 Tbsp paprika
- 1 Tbsp garlic powder
- 2 tsp ground ginger
- Sunflower or canola oil for brushing / dabbing on the chicken

Directions:
1. Make the day before. Mix the buttermilk, egg, and hot sauce in a bowl and then add it to a Ziploc bag with the chicken. Seal and lay this flat in a dish overnight in the fridge.
2. Take the chicken out of the fridge at least an hour before you want to cook it so that it comes up to room temperature. Mix all the ingredients for the flour coating in a bowl until well combined.
3. Get a tray set out and lined with baking/silicone paper.
4. Dredge the chicken in the following order: Take the chicken from the buttermilk into the flour mixture and toss to completely coat then set aside on the lined tray. You could dab/brush a little oil over the chicken at this stage and then proceed to the next step but first tossing it into the flour. Once all pieces are coated, quickly dip, and coat each piece 2 – 3 more times each. If some of the flour mixture clumps don't worry, try and press it onto the chicken.
5. Dab the top of each piece generously with olive oil. I used a silicone brush.
6. Preheat your Instant Vortex / Duo Crisp to 180C/350F. When it reaches temperature, spray the basket with non-stick cooking spray or olive oil / neutral oil spray. It's ok to use an aerosol spray if you have one. Or brush lightly with sunflower or canola oil.
7. Carefully place the chicken pieces in the basket and cook for 24 minutes. Turn them over halfway at 12 minutes. They should be golden brown and crunchy. Cook for a few extra minutes if you like them to be a darker colour. Serve with coleslaw or any other condiment of your choice.

Air Fryer Buffalo Chicken Livers With Blue Cheese Dipping Sauce
Servings: 4
Cooking Time: 8 Minutes
Ingredients:
- 1 cup (2 sticks) butter
- ½ cup   Hot Sauce
- 1 cup all-purpose flour
- 1 teaspoon salt
- ½ teaspoon paprika
- ½ teaspoon garlic powder
- ½ teaspoon cayenne pepper
- ½ teaspoon black pepper
- 1 pound chicken livers, soaked in milk
- oil, for spraying
- 1 cup blue cheese dressing
- 4 ounces blue cheese crumbled

Directions:
1. To make buffalo sauce, in a small saucepan, heat butter and The Lady & Sons Signature Hot Sauce until butter is just melted; keep warm until ready to use.
2. In a ziplock or paper bag, combine flour, salt, paprika, garlic powder, cayenne pepper, and black pepper. Place chicken livers in bag and shake gently until coated.
3. Working in batches of 10, spray each chicken liver with oil and place in air fryer basket. Do not overcrowd. Set temperature to 400 degrees, and air fry for 4 minutes. Turn livers, spray with oil, and air fry for 4 minutes more, or until golden brown. Transfer buffalo sauce to a large mixing bowl; in batches, immediately toss fried chicken livers in warm buffalo sauce. Repeat with remaining chicken livers.
4. To make dipping sauce, in a small bowl, stir together blue cheese dressing and crumbled blue cheese.

Air Fryer Chicken Legs
Servings: 4
Cooking Time: 18 Minutes

Ingredients:
- 8 to 10 bone-in, skin-on chicken legs/drumsticks (about 2 1/4 pounds)
- 1 tablespoon extra-virgin olive oil
- 1 tablespoon dark brown sugar
- 2 teaspoons smoked paprika
- 1 teaspoon kosher salt
- 1/2 teaspoon black pepper
- 1/2 teaspoon dry mustard powder
- 1/4 teaspoon ground cayenne pepper
- Chopped fresh cilantro or parsley or serving

Directions:
1. With paper towels, pat the chicken legs dry, and place in a large mixing bowl. Drizzle with the oil.
2. In a small bowl, stir together the brown sugar, smoked paprika, salt, pepper, mustard, and cayenne. Sprinkle over the chicken, then toss to evenly coat.
3. Preheat the air fryer to 400 degrees F, according to the manufacturer's instructions. Arrange a single layer of the drumsticks in the basket.
4. Air fry chicken legs for 10 minutes, then slide out the basket and flip the legs. Return to the air fryer and cook for 8 additional minutes, until the internal temperature of the chicken reaches at least 165 degrees F when a meat thermometer is inserted at the thickest part without touching the bone (I remove mine around 190 degrees F and it is still very juicy. The extra time ensures the skin is nice and crisp). Transfer to a plate and let rest 5 minutes. Serve hot, sprinkled with chopped cilantro or parsley as desired.

Notes
TO STORE: Refrigerate chicken in an airtight storage container for up to 4 days.
TO REHEAT: Gently rewarm leftovers on a baking sheet in the oven at 350 degrees F or in the microwave.
TO FREEZE: Freeze chicken in an airtight, freezer-safe storage container for up to 3 months. Let thaw overnight in the refrigerator before reheating.

Butter Chicken
Servings: 6
Cooking Time: 30 Minutes

Ingredients:
- 1 ½ pounds boneless, skinless chicken breast, cut into 1-inch pieces
- Kosher salt, as needed
- 3 tablespoons ghee
- ½ cup shallots, thinly sliced
- 1 can fire roasted crushed tomatoes (28 ounces)
- 1 ½ tablespoons fresh ginger, grated
- 6 garlic cloves, minced
- 1 tablespoons ground fenugreek
- 2 ½ teaspoons kosher salt, plus more as needed
- 2 teaspoon ground paprika
- 2 teaspoons turmeric
- 1 teaspoon ground cumin

- ½ teaspoon ground cardamom
- ¼ teaspoon ground cloves
- 1/3 cup cashew butter
- 1 cup chicken stock
- 1 can coconut milk (15 ounces)
- 2 tablespoons fresh cilantro, chopped, for serving
- Warm naan bread, for serving
- Items Needed:
- Blender

Directions:
1. Season the chicken generously with kosher salt.
2. Select the Sauté Function on the Pressure Cooker and press Temp Set, then customize the temperature to high and time to 12 minutes.
3. Add 2 tablespoons of ghee into the pressure cooker, then sear off the chicken in batches, removing the chicken to a plate as each piece is golden brown on all sides.
4. Add the remaining ghee and the shallots into the inner pot and cook, stirring occasionally, until the shallots are translucent, then stir in the garlic, ginger, and spices, followed by the cashew butter. Pour in the tomatoes and chicken stock stir to dissolve the cashew butter, then add the chicken pieces back into the pot.
5. Place the lid onto the pressure cooker.
6. Select the Pressure function, adjust pressure to high, and time to 15 minutes, then press Start.
7. Slowly release pressure by sliding the vent switch in between Seal and Vent. Slide the switch to Vent after 15 minutes.
8. Open the lid carefully.
9. Stir the coconut milk into the sauce, then adjust the seasoning to taste with kosher salt.
10. Serve the butter chicken on plates with naan, garnished with cilantro.

Air-fryer Chicken Tenders

Servings: 4
Cooking Time: 15 Minutes

Ingredients:
- 1/2 cup panko bread crumbs
- 1/2 cup potato sticks, crushed
- 1/2 cup crushed cheese crackers
- 1/4 cup grated Parmesan cheese
- 2 bacon strips, cooked and crumbled
- 2 teaspoons minced fresh chives
- 1/4 cup butter, melted
- 1 tablespoon sour cream
- 1 pound chicken tenderloins
- Additional sour cream and chives

Directions:
1. Preheat air fryer to 400°. In a shallow bowl, combine the first 6 ingredients. In another shallow bowl, whisk butter and sour cream. Dip chicken in butter mixture, then in crumb mixture, patting to help coating adhere.
2. In batches, arrange chicken in a single layer on greased tray in air-fryer basket; spritz with cooking spray. Cook until coating is golden brown and chicken is no longer pink, 7-8 minutes on each side. Serve with additional sour cream and chives.

Crispy Air Fryer Fried Chicken Breast

Servings: 4
Cooking Time: 10 Minutes

Ingredients:
- 2 boneless skinless chicken breasts sliced into thin cutlets
- 1 Tablespoon olive oil
- ½ cup panko bread crumbs
- ½ cup dried bread crumbs
- ¼ teaspoon cayenne pepper
- ½ teaspoon garlic powder
- 1/2 teaspoon onion powder
- ½ teaspoon ground black pepper
- ½ teaspoon white pepper
- 1 teaspoon olive oil spray

Directions:
1. Coat both sides of the chicken with an even coating of olive oil.

2. In a rimmed dish, combine the bread crumbs, panko, and seasonings.
3. Coat each piece of chicken with the seasoned bread crumbs. Spray each breaded chicken breast with a light coat of olive oil.
4. Place the chicken breasts into a single layer into the air fryer basket.
5. Air fry chicken at 390 degrees Fahreheit for 10-12 minutes, flipping the chicken halfway through the cooking time.
6. Carefully remove the chicken from the air fryer and serve immediately.

NOTES

Use a different cut of chicken - This recipe can be made with chicken thighs, chicken drumsticks, and any other chicken pieces that you want.

Add brown sugar - If you want to make the boneless skinless chicken breast a little sweet, adding a little sugar will be perfect.

Spice things up by adding a little chili powder.

For extra crispy chicken, soak the chicken in a buttermilk mixture with egg for about 30 minutes to an hour before breading. Add a light coat of flour mixture before dipping it into egg and then seasoned breadcrumbs. Spray with olive oil before air frying.

How to make Unbreaded Fried Chicken in the Air Fryer

Coat both sides of the chicken with an even coating of olive oil.

In a rimmed dish or shallow bowl, combine the seasonings.

Coat each piece of chicken with the seasonings.

Once seasoned, spray each breaded chicken breast with a light coat of olive oil.

Place the chicken breasts into a single layer into the air fryer basket.

Air fry chicken at 390 degrees Fahrenheit for 10-12 minutes, flipping the chicken halfway through the cooking time.

Carefully remove the chicken from the air fryer and serve immediately.

Crispy Sesame Chicken

Ingredients:
- 1kg chicken pieces of your choice
- (I used drumsticks and chicken fillet)
- Salt and Pepper for seasoning
- 3 tablespoons cornflour
- 3 eggs
- 3 cups flour
- 3 tablespoons barbecue spice
- 3 teaspoon paprika
- 3 tablespoons sesame seeds
- 1 tablespoon mixed herbs
- Olive oil spray

Directions:
1. Cut the chicken fillets into strips and make 2 slits across the top of the drumsticks. In a medium bowl whisk together the egg with a dash of milk.
2. In a separate large bowl add together the flour spices, herbs and sesame seeds. Mix until well combined. Line a tray with baking paper or cling wrap. Rinse the chicken and pat dry with roller towel, season with salt and pepper and dust with the cornflour. Dip the chicken in the beaten egg and then in the flour mixture and transfer to the lined tray. Once all the chicken is evenly coated, transfer to the tray. Pop the chicken in the freezer for 20 minutes and allow the coating to set. (If you resting chicken for longer than 20 minutes pop the chicken in the fridge and not freezer)
3. After 20 minutes spray both sides of the chicken with olive oil and air fry in the Vortex Air fryer on 200 degrees for 15-20 minutes, turning halfway.
4. NB: To maximize crispness, do not overcrowd the basket, rather fry in 2 batches but leave enough space in between the chicken to crisp to perfection.
5. Enjoy!

BREAKFAST & BRUNCH RECIPES

Cheese & Veggie Egg Cups

Ingredients:
- 4 eggs, large
- 1 cup veggies of your choice, diced
- 1 cup shredded cheese
- 4 tbsp half and half
- 1 tbsp cilantro, chopped
- salt and pepper, for sprinkling
- cooking spray

Directions:
1. Grease your air fryer safe muffin tin and set aside.
2. In a medium mixing bowl, whisk together the eggs, vegetables, half the cheese, half and half, cilantro, salt and pepper together.
3. Divide the mixture evenly into each cup of the muffin tin and place it in the air fryer. Air fry at 300°F for 12 minutes. Then, top the cups with the remaining cheese and air fry at 400°F for another 1-2 minutes, or until lightly browned.
4. Serve immediately and enjoy!

Air Fryer Copycat Starbucks Banana Bread

Servings: 8
Cooking Time: 30 Minutes

Ingredients:
- 2 cups all-purpose flour
- 1 teaspoon baking soda
- 1/2 teaspoon salt
- 1 large egg
- 1 1/4 cup granulated sugar
- 1/2 cup vegetable oil
- 2 tablespoons milk
- 1 teaspoon pure vanillla extract
- 3 large ripe bananas
- 1/2 cup diced walnuts optional

Directions:
1. Start by making the mix. In a large mixing bowl, mix the flour, baking soda, salt, egg, and sugar.
2. Then mix in the oil, milk, and vanilla. Mix well.
3. Add the bananas.
4. Mix until smooth. If using walnuts, stir the walnuts in now.
5. Pour the prepared batter into a prepared air fryer-safe pan that has been coated with non-stick cooking spray.
6. Set the temperature to 310 F and the time for 30 minutes. After 30 minutes, check and check for doneness. If it is not done, add another 5 minutes. Until it's fully cooked and a toothpick comes out clean.
7. Once fully cooked, remove the loaf pan from the air fryer basket, and let it cool slightly.
8. Once cooled, slice and serve.
9. Plate, serve, and enjoy!

Air Fryer Hard Boiled Eggs

Servings: 6
Cooking Time: 15 Minutes

Ingredients:
- 6 large eggs

Directions:
1. Place baking rack in the bowl in the low position. Carefully place eggs on top.
2. Tap the bake button and set temperature to 300°F and fry for 12-14 minutes.
3. Note: 12 minutes for a looser yolk. 14 minutes for a set yolk.
4. Carefully move eggs, with tongs, to a bowl of cold water for 5-10 minutes.
5. Tap eggs on a hard surface and peel.
6. Store in an airtight container in the refrigerator for 3-4 days.

Air Fryer Hash Browns

Servings: 2
Cooking Time: 18 Minutes

Ingredients:
- 2 cups grated Yukon potatoes
- 1/4 teaspoon paprika
- 1/4 teaspoon garlic powder
- 1/4 teaspoon kosher salt
- 1/8 teaspoon black pepper
- Nonstick spray
- Chives or parsley, garnish

Directions:
1. Peel and grate the potatoes:
2. Peel the potatoes and grate them with a box grater on the large holes.
3. Rinse the potatoes:
4. Add the grated potatoes to a bowl with cold water. Rinse the potatoes a few times until the water is mostly clean. Drain off as much water as possible from the potatoes.
5. Alternatively, you can rinse the potatoes in a colander, but some potatoes might slip through the colander holes!
6. Dry the potatoes:
7. Remove the potatoes from the bowl and spread them out over a few paper towels and dry them well.
8. Season the potatoes:
9. Then add grated potatoes to a large bowl and season with paprika, garlic powder, salt, and pepper. Stir with a spoon to season evenly.
10. Air fry the hash browns:
11. Spray an air fryer basket with nonstick spray.
12. Spread out the hash browns in the basket of an air fryer in an even layer. Then spritz the hash browns with a little nonstick spray. It's okay if they overlap or stack up some.
13. Close the air fryer basket and air fry the hash browns for 8 minutes at 350°F.
14. Stir the hash browns:
15. Open the air fryer basket and stir the potatoes gently using a wooden spoon so they cook evenly. If there are any clumps of potatoes, try to break them up. The potatoes might start to take on some color on the edges, which is good!
16. Finish cooking the hash browns:
17. Close the basket again and then air fry them a second time for 6-8 minutes until they are very crispy.
18. To serve:
19. Divide hash browns between plates and serve with eggs and sprinkled with fresh chives or parsley.

Air Fryer Bacon And Egg Breakfast Biscuit Bombs

Servings: 10

Ingredients:
- Biscuit Bombs
- 4 slices bacon, cut into 1/2-inch pieces
- 1 tablespoon butter
- 2 eggs, beaten
- 1/4 teaspoon pepper
- 1 can (10.2 oz) refrigerated Pillsbury™ Grands!™ Southern Homestyle Buttermilk Biscuits (5 Count)
- 2 oz sharp cheddar cheese, cut into ten 3/4-inch cubes
- Egg Wash
- 1 egg
- 1 tablespoon water

Directions:
1. Cut two 8-inch rounds of cooking parchment paper. Place one round in bottom of air fryer basket. Spray with cooking spray.
2. In 10-inch nonstick skillet, cook bacon over medium-high heat until crisp. Remove from pan; place on paper towel. Carefully wipe skillet with paper towel. Add butter to skillet; melt over medium heat. Add 2 beaten eggs and pepper to skillet; cook until eggs are thickened but still moist, stirring frequently. Remove from heat; stir in bacon. Cool 5 minutes.
3. Meanwhile, separate dough into 5 biscuits; separate each biscuit into 2 layers. Press each into 4-inch round. Spoon 1 heaping

tablespoonful egg mixture onto center of each round. Top with one piece of the cheese. Gently fold edges up and over filling; pinch to seal. In small bowl, beat remaining egg and water. Brush biscuits on all sides with egg wash.
4. Place 5 of the biscuit bombs, seam sides down, on parchment in air fryer basket. Spray both sides of second parchment round with cooking spray. Top biscuit bombs in basket with second parchment round, then top with remaining 5 biscuit bombs.
5. Set to 325°F; cook 8 minutes. Remove top parchment round; using tongs, carefully turn biscuits, and place in basket in single layer. Cook 4 to 6 minutes longer or until cooked through (at least 165°F).

Air Fryer Garlic Bread
Servings: 4
Cooking Time: 6 Minutes
Ingredients:
- Half loaf of bread
- 3 tablespoons butter, softened
- 3 garlic cloves, minced
- 1/2 teaspoon dried Italian seasoning
- small pinch of red pepper flakes

Directions:
1. Preheat your air fryer to 350 degrees.
2. Cut the bread in half or sized to fit your air fryer.
3. Mix the butter, garlic, Italian seasoning, and red pepper flakes in a small bowl.
4. Baste the garlic butter mixture on top of the bread evenly.
5. Place the garlic bread in the air fryer side by side and cook for 6 to 7 minutes until browned to your liking.

Air Fryer Frozen Burritos
Servings: 4
Cooking Time: 10 Minutes
Ingredients:
- 4 burritos frozen

Directions:
1. Preheat your Air Fryer to 400 degrees Fahrenheit or 200 degrees Celcius. Prepare the air fryer basket.
2. Place the frozen burritos in air fryer basket.
3. Air fry at the frozen burritos at 400 degrees Fahrenheit for 12-15 minutes. Make sure to flip the burritos several times during the cooking process.

NOTES
What toppings go well with burritos?
Literally, anything that you're wanting. I love to add a bit of hot sauce to the outside of the crispy tortilla and I really make sure to over the outside of the burrito with sour cream and chives as well. Don't forget to top with a bit of lime juice as well!

Air Fryer French Onion Corn On The Cob
Servings: 4
Cooking Time: 25 Minutes
Ingredients:
- 4 corn on the cob
- mayonnaise, to taste
- French onion soup mix, to taste
- dry ranch dressing mix, to taste
- garlic powder, to taste
- black pepper , to taste
- paprika, to taste

Directions:
1. Mix all ingredients, except the corn, together in a bowl. Coat each cob with the mixture and individually
2. wrap each one in aluminum foil. Air fry it at 350°F for 20-25 minutes.
3. You can also bake it in the oven at 375°F for 25 minutes or grill it until the corn is tender.

Air Fryer Hash Brown Egg Bites
Servings: 7
Ingredients:
- Deselect All
- Nonstick cooking spray, for the mold
- 4 large eggs
- 1/4 cup heavy cream
- Kosher salt
- 2/3 cup shredded Cheddar
- 1/4 cup diced red bell peppers
- 1 scallion, white and green parts sliced
- 1/2 cup shredded frozen hash browns, thawed

Directions:
1. Special equipment: a 7-cavity silicone egg bites mold, 6-quart air fryer
2. Spray the cavities of a 7-cavity silicone egg bites mold with nonstick spray. Whisk together the eggs, heavy cream and 1/2 teaspoon salt in a large glass measuring cup until no white streaks remain.
3. Divide the egg mixture, 1/3 cup of the Cheddar, the bell peppers and scallions among the cavities of the mold. Gently stir the mixture in each cavity with a spoon. Transfer the mold to the basket of a 6-quart air fryer, set it to 300°F and cook for 3 minutes.
4. Meanwhile, combine the hash browns and remaining 1/3 cup Cheddar in a small bowl. Gently top each egg bite with the hash brown-cheese mixture.
5. Set the air fryer to 300°F and cook for 12 minutes more. The top of each bite should be golden brown and the eggs should be set. Remove the mold and let stand for 10 minutes before popping out the egg bites. Serve warm.

Air Fryer Avocado Eggs
Servings: 2
Cooking Time: 8 Minutes
Ingredients:
- 2 avocados
- 4 eggs
- salt and pepper to taste
- toppings optional: Salsa, Shredded Cheese, Crumbled Bacon, Hot Sauce

Directions:
1. Line the air fryer basket with parchment paper and set aside.
2. Slice avocado in half, lengthwise, and then carefully remove the pit.
3. Using a spoon, gently remove some of the avocado meat, forming a well where the pit was. Save the removed avocado to top the egg, or to eat separately.
4. Place halves in the air fryer basket, and then carefully crack eggs, breaking direction into each half of the avocado.
5. Air fry at 400 degrees F for 8-12 minutes, depending on how well done you prefer your eggs.
6. Season as desired.

NOTES
Variations
Make an avocado toast - If you want to spread the cooked cream avocado on toast and add a bit of Bagel seasoning, you can create an avocado mixture on bread in no time at all. Simple ingredients can easily make all sorts of an easy breakfast.

Add feta cheese - Putting feta cheese on top of the fried egg sounds awesome. This is a simple way that you can make air fryer-baked eggs with an avocado half taste different easily.

Make it spicy - Add some sweet chili sauce to the top of avocado eggs for a spicy hot flavor combination. You can skip the sweet and add red pepper flakes as well.

Pair with other breakfast foods - Make it a large meal by adding some hash browns, turkey bacon, or even fresh fruit.

Air Fryer Pizza Egg Rolls

Servings: 4
Cooking Time: 10 Minutes

Ingredients:
- 8 egg roll wrappers
- 8 mozzarella cheese sticks
- pepperoni slices
- ¼ cup pizza sauce

Directions:
1. Lay out wrappers with corners left and right. Add a small spoonful of pizza sauce onto the center of the eggroll wrapper.
2. Add 3-4 slices of pepperonis, overlapping pieces, then top with a mozzarella cheese stick. Fold bottom corn over the filling and tuck under.
3. Next, fold in the left and right corners, and then turn over, to make a large pillow shape.
4. Lightly spray the air fryer basket, and place each Egg Roll in the basket without stacking or overlapping. Lightly spray each egg roll to help with crispness and color.
5. Air fry at 400 degrees F for 10-12 minutes, until golden and crispy. Turn halfway during the air frying process.
6. Serve with marinara or pizza sauce for dipping. Garnish with parsley flakes.

NOTES
Variations
Add different ingredients - Don't forget that you can easily add your favorite pizza toppings to the middle of these golden brown egg rolls. You can make cheese pizza egg rolls only, or add extra pizza sauce, turkey pepperoni, diced green pepper, black olives, or any other different flavors that you want to add.

Air Fryer Frozen Hash Brown Patties

Servings: 4
Cooking Time: 15 Minutes

Ingredients:
- 4 Frozen Hash Brown Patties
- salt , optional to taste
- black pepper , optional to taste
- EQUIPMENT
- Air Fryer

Directions:
1. Place the frozen hash brown patties in the air fryer basket and spread in an even layer (make sure they aren't overlapping). No oil spray is needed.
2. Air Fry at 380°F/193°C for 10 minutes. Flip the hashbrown patties over.
3. Continue to Air Fry at 380°F/193°C for an additional 2-5 minutes or until crisped to your liking. Season with salt & pepper, if desired.

NOTES
Air Frying Tips and Notes:
No Oil Necessary. Cook Frozen - Do not thaw first.
Turn as needed. Cook in a single layer in the air fryer basket.
Recipe timing is based on a non-preheated air fryer. If cooking in multiple batches back to back, the following batches may cook a little quicker.
Recipes were tested in 3.7 to 6 qt. air fryers. If using a larger air fryer, the hash browns might cook quicker so adjust cooking time.
Remember to set a timer to flip as directed in recipe.

Air Fryer German Pancake Bites

Ingredients:
- Pancakes:
- 6 eggs
- 1 cup whole milk
- 1 tsp salt
- 1 cup all-purpose flour
- Toppings Options:
- Chocolate hazelnut spread
- Berries
- Banana slices

Directions:
1. In a large bowl, beat together eggs and milk. Sift in flour and salt. MIx well with electric mixer and set aside.

2. Lightly butter ramekins or 4 small oven-safe cups. Fill each container 1/4 full of batter.
3. Place in air fryer and set to 400F for 6 minutes.
4. Carefully remove pancake bites from ramekins and top with your favorite toppings!
5. Enjoy!

Air Fryer "pretzel" Bites & Irish Pub Beer Cheese

Servings: 6

Ingredients:
- Pretzel Bites:
- 1 can prepared biscuits
- 8 cups water
- ⅓ cup baking soda
- ¼ cup butter, melted
- 2 tablespoons flaky salt or pretzel salt
- Items Needed:
- Slotted spoon
- Food processor fitted with blade attachment
- Small heatproof baking dish
- Beer Cheese:
- 6 ounces cream cheese
- 1 cup sharp cheddar cheese, freshly shredded
- 1 cup Irish cheddar cheese, freshly shredded
- 1 cup Fontina cheese, freshly shredded
- ⅔ cup stout beer
- 3 garlic cloves, minced
- 1 tablespoon spicy brown mustard
- 1½ teaspoons Worcestershire sauce
- 1 teaspoon paprika
- 1 teaspoon kosher salt
- 1 tablespoon fresh chives, chopped, for garnish

Directions:
1. Cut the individual biscuits into quarters and roll into balls. Set aside.
2. Bring the water to a boil in a large saucepan and add the baking soda. Boil the biscuit dough balls for 15 to 20 seconds at a time, then transfer to a tray using a slotted spoon.
3. Place the crisper plate into the Smart Air Fryer basket, then place the boiled dough balls onto the crisper plate in a single layer.
4. Brush the dough balls with melted butter and sprinkle with flaky salt or pretzel salt.
5. Select the Air Fry function, adjust time to 10 minutes, then press Start/Pause. Open the basket to brush the pretzel bites with butter every 3 to 4 minutes.
6. Remove the pretzel bites when done.
7. Place the cream cheese and all three shredded cheeses into the bowl of a food processor fitted with the blade attachment. Blend until fully combined.
8. Add the beer, garlic, mustard, Worcestershire sauce, paprika, and salt into the food processor and blend until smooth.
9. Transfer the cheese into a small heatproof baking dish.
10. Place the baking dish onto the crisper plate.
11. Select the Broil function, adjust time to 5 minutes, then press Start/Pause.
12. Remove the beer cheese when done, garnish with chives, and serve with the pretzel bites.

Air Fryer Egg Bites

Servings: 7
Cooking Time: 15 Minutes

Ingredients:
- 7 eggs
- 1 tablespoon heavy cream
- ¼ cup cheddar cheese shredded
- 4 slices bacon pre-cooked and chopped
- 1 tablespoon milk
- 2 green onions sliced
- ¼ teaspoon mustard powder
- salt and pepper to taste

Directions:
1. Preheat air fryer to 340°F.
2. Whisk eggs, cream, mustard powder, salt & pepper in a medium bowl until fluffy and pale yellow in color.
3. Divide bacon, cheese and green onions over the cups of the molds (or small bowls).

4. Place in the air fryer basket and pour egg mixture overtop.
5. Cook in the air fryer for 11-13 minutes stirring after 7-8 minutes. Cook just until eggs are set (they will continue cooking a little bit once removed. Rest 5 minutes before serving.

Notes

Air Fryers can vary. Based on your appliance and the size of the mold you use, the eggs may need a little bit more or less time. Cook just until they are set.

Whisk the eggs until they're a fluffy pale yellow. You should see no bits of white or yolk.

Don't add too many mix-ins or the egg bites won't hold together.

If adding veggies, precook them and squeeze out any moisture before adding.

Stir the eggs after 7 or 8 minutes. This helps distribute the add ins (or they will sink or float depending on what you've added).

Eggs will continue to cook after they've been removed from the air fryer so do not overcook.

Air Fryer Zucchini Pizza Bites

Servings: 4
Cooking Time: 10 Minutes

Ingredients:
- 2 zucchini (medium sized)
- ¾ cup Primal Kitchen's Roasted Garlic Marinara Sauce
- ¾ cup shredded mozzarella cheese
- ½ cup turkey pepperoni
- 1 tbsp olive oil (for spraying)

Directions:
1. Slice the zucchini into slices that are about ¼ inch thick.
2. Lay the zucchini slices flat in the air fryer basket. Do not overcrowd. The zucchini should not overlap. You will need to do this in batches. Spray the slices with olive oil and cook for 3-4 minutes at 400 degrees F.
3. Add the marinara sauce, shredded mozzarella cheese and turkey pepperoni on top of each zucchini slice.
4. Place the basket back into the air fryer and cook for 4-6 minutes at 400 degrees F or until the cheese melts.
5. Repeat as many times as needed depending on the size of your air fryer. As you are making them, let them cool on a wire cooling rack.

Air Fryer Baked Oats

Ingredients:
- 1 cup oats
- 1/2cup milk of choice
- 1 tablespoon lemon curd flavoured yogurt
- 1 teaspoon baking powder
- 1 banana
- 1 flat teaspoon cinnamon
- 2 teaspoon honey
- 5/6 raspberries
- Dark choc chips

Directions:
1. In a blender blend all your ingredients besides the raspberries and choc chips. Until it's a smooth paste. Pour into ramekins. Top with raspberries and choc chips. Place into your Vortex air fryer to bake on 160 degrees Celsius for 10 minutes then turn to 180 for 2 more minutes.
2. I added a dollop of lemon curd yogurt to the top. This feels like a dessert or baked pudding for breakfast. You can use any variety of toppings and additions, you could use plain yoghurt I just love the combination of raspberries and lemon.

Air Fryer Soft Boiled Eggs

Servings: 4
Cooking Time: 6 Minutes

Ingredients:
- 4 large eggs

Directions:
1. Place the eggs in a small ramekin or silicone dish, or in the air fryer basket.
2. Air fry at 300 degrees F for 6-8 minutes. (Six minutes for very runny yolks and

whites, 8 minutes for more firm whites, but still slightly runny yolks)
3. When done air frying, place eggs into an ice bath until they are warm to the touch. Gently peel eggs and serve as desired.
4. If using eggs as "dippy eggs," place slightly cooled eggs in egg holders, and gently crack tops with a spoon, and remove the top shells.

Air Fryer Cauliflower Tacos
Servings: 4
Ingredients:
- FOR THE SLAW
- 1 c. thinly sliced red cabbage
- 1/2 small red onion, diced
- 1 jalapeño, minced
- 1 clove garlic, minced
- Juice of 1 lime
- 2 tbsp. apple cider vinegar
- Pinch kosher salt
- FOR THE CAULIFLOWER
- 1 1/2 c. all-purpose flour
- 1 tsp. chili powder
- 1 tsp. cumin
- 1/2 tsp. garlic powder
- 1/2 tsp. cayenne pepper
- Kosher salt
- Freshly ground black pepper
- 1 1/2 c. almond milk or other non-dairy milk
- 1 1/2 c. panko bread crumbs
- 1 medium head cauliflower, cut into bite-size florets
- Cooking spray
- FOR SERVING
- 1/2 c. vegan mayonnaise
- 2 tbsp. sriracha
- 1 tsp. maple syrup
- Corn tortillas
- Sliced avocado
- Freshly chopped cilantro
- Lime wedges

Directions:

1. In a medium bowl, combine slaw ingredients. Let sit while prepping tacos, stirring every so often.
2. In a medium bowl, combine flour and spices and season well with salt and pepper. Add almond milk and stir to combine. Mixture should be thick, but still easy to dip cauliflower into. Add a little more milk if needed. Place panko into small bowl.
3. Dip florets into milk mixture, wiping any excess off, then toss in panko.
4. Working in batches, place coated cauliflower into basket of air fryer and spray with cooking spray. Cook at 400° for 15 minutes, stopping about halfway through to toss and spray with more cooking spray.
5. In a small bowl, combine vegan mayonnaise, sriracha, and maple syrup.
6. Assemble tacos: On a tortilla top with cooked cauliflower, avocado, pickled slaw, cilantro, and a drizzle of sriracha mayo. Serve with lime wedges.

Air Fryer Pasta Tacos
Servings: 4
Cooking Time: 45 Minutes
Ingredients:
- 24 jumbo pasta shells
- 60ml (1/4 cup) extra virgin olive oil
- 1 small red onion, chopped
- 500g beef mince
- 2 tsp ground cumin
- 2 tsp ground coriander
- 1 tsp garlic powder
- 375g jar medium thick 'n' chunky salsa
- 125g can black beans
- 1 1/2 tsp Mexican chilli powder
- 80g (1 cup) grated cheddar
- 2 tomatoes, diced
- 1 avocado, diced
- Fresh coriander sprigs, to serve
- Sour cream, to serve
- Lime cheeks, to serve
- Select all ingredients

Directions:
1. Cook pasta in a large saucepan of boiling, salted water for 10 minutes or until just tender. Using a slotted spoon, transfer pasta to a tray lined with paper towel to drain.
2. Meanwhile, heat half the oil in a large frying pan over medium-high heat. Add onion. Cook, stirring for 5 minutes or until softened. Add mince. Cook, breaking up mince with a wooden spoon, for 5 minutes or until browned. Add cumin, coriander and half the garlic powder. Cook, stirring for 1 minute or until fragrant. Add salsa and beans. Season with salt and pepper. Bring to a simmer. Reduce heat to low. Simmer for 15 minutes.
3. Preheat air fryer on 200C. Combine Mexican chilli powder, remaining garlic powder and oil in a large bowl. Add pasta. Season well with salt and pepper. Toss gently to coat. Spoon mince mixture in pasta shells to fill. Sprinkle with cheese. Place 1/3 of the pasta shells, cheese-side up, in the air fryer basket. Cook for 5-8 minutes or until shells are golden and crispy. Carefully transfer to a large serving plate. Repeat with remaining pasta.
4. Top with combined tomato and avocado. Sprinkle with coriander. Serve with sour cream and lime cheeks.

Air Fryer Ham And Swiss Crescent Rolls

Servings: 4

Ingredients:
- 1 can (8 oz) refrigerated Pillsbury™ Original Crescent Rolls (8 Count)
- 8 thin slices deli ham (3.5 oz)
- 4 thin slices Swiss cheese (3 oz), each cut into 4 strips

Directions:
1. Cut 8-inch round of cooking parchment paper; place in bottom of air fryer basket.
2. Unroll dough; separate into 8 triangles. Place 1 piece of ham on each triangle; place 2 strips of cheese down center of ham. Fold in edges of ham to match shape of dough triangle. Roll up each crescent, ending at tip of triangle.
3. On parchment paper in air fryer basket, place 4 crescent rolls point sides down. Cover remaining crescent rolls with plastic wrap, and refrigerate.
4. Set air fryer to 300°F; cook 6 minutes. With tongs, turn over each one; cook 4 to 7 minutes longer or until golden brown. Remove from air fryer. Repeat with remaining 4 crescent rolls. Serve warm.

Air Fryer Mickey Cinnamon Rolls

Servings: 4
Cooking Time: 8 Minutes

Ingredients:
- 1 can refrigerated cinnamon roll dough

Directions:
1. To begin open the can of cinnamon rolls and separate the eight rolls. Set aside four of the rolls. Unroll the remaining four and then cut them in half.
2. Tightly re-roll each piece back into a circular shape and press both halves on top of a whole cinnamon roll, making ears.
3. Pinch the dough together so the ears and had become one piece and won't separate during the cooking process.
4. Place in the air fryer basket or on baking sheet, after lightly spring with a nonstick cooking spray or lining with air fryer parchment paper. Leave enough room in between the cinnamon rolls so they don't overlap or touch.
5. Air Fry at 360 degrees for 8-10 minutes until golden brown. Remove from the air fryer basket and allowed to slightly cool for 1-2 minutes, then drizzle the frosting glaze on top of cinnamon rolls.

Air Fryer French Toast Sticks

Servings: 4
Cooking Time: 10 Minutes

Ingredients:
- 5 slices of bread
- 2 eggs
- 1/3 cup milk
- 3 tablespoons sugar
- 2 tablespoons flour
- 1 teaspoon ground cinnamon
- 1/2 teaspoon vanilla extract
- 1/8 teaspoon salt
- OPTIONAL
- Confectioners sugar for dusting
- Maple syrup for dipping

Directions:
1. Preheat your air fryer to 370 degrees.
2. Cut each piece of bread into 3 equal pieces and set aside.
3. Put the eggs, milk, flour, sugar, vanilla, ground cinnamon, and salt into a wide shallow dish. Whisk to combine.
4. Dip each piece of bread into the egg mixture, making sure to coat on all sides.
5. Place a piece of parchment round paper inside the air fryer and place each french toast stick in one single layer on top of the parchment round (needed to prevent sticking).
6. Cook for about 10 minutes, flipping halfway through.
7. Carefully remove the air fryer french toast sticks from the air fryer and enjoy immediately, store in the fridge for up to 3 days, or freeze up to 3 months.

NOTES
HOW TO REHEAT FRENCH TOAST STICKS IN THE AIR FRYER:
Preheat your air fryer to 350 degrees.
Cook french toast sticks for 2-3 minutes until warmed and enjoy!
HOW TO COOK FROZEN FRENCH TOAST STICKS IN THE AIR FRYER:
Preheat your air fryer to 320 degrees.
Cook frozen french toast sticks in the air fryer for 2-3 minutes until warmed and enjoy!

Crispy Spinach Tacos

Servings: 9
Cooking Time: 20 Minutes

Ingredients:
- 9 small spinach tortillas (5-inch diameter)
- 2 cups of (360 g) cooked rice
- 1 (15 oz) can kidney beans or black beans (rinsed and drained)
- 1 small/medium onion diced
- ½ tbsp oil
- 2 garlic cloves minced
- ½ bell pepper chopped
- ¾ cup (100 g) canned mushrooms or use fresh
- ½ tsp onion powder
- ½ tsp ground cumin
- ½ tsp paprika
- ¼ tsp smoked paprika
- ¼ tsp ground ginger (optional)
- ¼ tsp black pepper or more to taste
- sea salt to taste
- 1 tbsp balsamic vinegar
- 1 tbsp soy sauce (gluten-free if needed)
- 4 tbsp plant-based milk
- ⅓ cup (80 g) passata
- 2 tbsp hot sauce (or use less/more to taste)
- 1 batch (200 g) vegan cheese sauce or use 7 oz store-bought vegan cheese

Directions:
1. Cook rice according to package instructions. You will need 2 cups of cooked rice for this recipe.
2. Prepare the spinach tortillas (click for the recipe) or use store-bought flour tortillas or corn tortillas of choice.
3. Meanwhile, heat oil in a pan/skillet over medium heat and add the onion, mushrooms, and bell pepper.
4. Sauté for about 3-5 minutes, then add garlic for a further minute. Stir occasionally.
5. Add all spices, balsamic vinegar, soy sauce, plant-based milk, passata, and hot sauce. Stir and let simmer for about 3 minutes.
6. Add cooked rice and beans, stir and turn off the heat.
7. Taste and adjust seasoning if needed.

8. Preheat oven to 410 degrees Fahrenheit (210 degrees Celsius) and line a baking sheet with parchment paper.
9. Make one batch of the vegan cheese sauce or use store-bought vegan cheese.
10. Add about 2 tbsp of the rice filling on one side of a tortilla and 1 tbsp of the vegan cheese. Fold the other side over the filling and press it slightly down with your fingers (see pictures above in the blog post). Do the same for the remaining tortillas.
11. Transfer all tortillas to the baking sheet. Bake in the oven for about 10-15 minutes, or until crispy. Enjoy hot!
12. Check the blog post for the air-fryer method.

Air Fryer Lasagna Egg Rolls

Servings: 15
Cooking Time: 30 Minutes

Ingredients:
- 3 cups (710 ml) cooked lasagna, cooled
- 1 cup (112 g) shredded mozzarella cheese
- 15 (15) egg roll wrappers
- water, for sealing the wrappers
- oil spray, for coating the egg rolls
- 1/2-1 cup (120-240 ml) dipping sauce of choice, marinara, ranch, bbq sauce, etc.
- EQUIPMENT
- Air Fryer

Directions:
1. Cook the lasagna and then let cool to at least room temperature or use leftover lasagna. Cut into small slices about 2 Tablespoons in volume.
2. Using egg roll wrappers or spring roll wrappers, add the 2 Tablespoons piece of the lasagna filling to each wrapper. Add about 2 teaspoons of shredded cheese on top. Tuck and roll the wrapper around the filling (watch the video in the post above to see how to roll even and tight rolls). Brush the top corner of the wrapper with water to help seal the wrapper end, and then finish rolling the egg roll. Repeat for all the egg rolls.
3. Brush or spray rolls with oil to coat. Place egg rolls in a single layer in the air fryer basket (cook in batches).
4. Air Fry 380°F for 12-16 minutes, flipping halfway through. Cook until the wrapper is crispy and browned. If you use the larger wrapper or if your wrappers are thicker cook a little longer so that all the layers can cook through to avoid being tough and chewy.
5. Allow to cool a little (the filling will be super hot right after cooking), and then serve with your favorite dipping sauce.

FAVORITE AIR FRYER RECIPES

3 Cheese Air Fryer Mini Pizzas
Cooking Time: 4 Minutes

Ingredients:
- 1 can biscuits
- ⅓ cup pizza sauce
- ⅓ cup mozzarella cheese shredded
- ⅓ cup cheddar cheese shredded
- 2 tablespoon parmesan cheese grated

Directions:
1. Preheat air fryer to 400°F.
2. Roll out the biscuits into flat circles.
3. Top with the pizza sauce and cheese.
4. Place in the air fryer basket and cook for 4 minutes or until cheese is melted.

Air Fryer Jalepeno Poppers
Servings: 6
Cooking Time: 12 Minutes

Ingredients:
- 6 medium Jalapeños
- 4 ounces cream cheese, softened
- 6-12 slices bacon

Directions:
1. Cut the jalapeños in half, lengthwise. Remove all of the seeds and rinse the jalapeños.
2. Cut small slices of the cream cheese, in strips, and place a strip inside each half piece of the pepper.
3. Wrap a piece of bacon around the stuffed pepper and secure with a toothpick.
4. Place the stuffed peppers in the basket of the air fryer, working in batches if necessary. Be sure they aren't overlapping each other in the basket.
5. Cook at 370 degrees Fahrenheit for 10-12 minutes, until the bacon is cooked to your desired crispness.

NOTES
If you use smaller jalapeños, cut the bacon slices in half before wrapping the pepper. If the cream cheese is chilled, it is easier to cut into strips.
This recipe makes 12 poppers, with a serving of three poppers per person.

Air Fryer Fried Rice

Ingredients:
- 3 cups rice cooked and cold
- 1 cup frozen mixed vegetables
- 1 tbsp oyster sauce
- 1 tsp sesame oil
- 2 eggs scrambled
- 2 tbsp choppled green onion tops

Directions:
1. To make your air fryer fried rice, put your cold rice into an large bowl.
2. Mix in the frozen vegetables to the bowl of rice.
3. Add the scrambled eggs into the rice and vegetables.
4. Add the sesame oil and oyster sauce. Mix well until fully combined.
5. Transfer the rice mixture to an oven safe container like a ramekin.
6. Place that container into your air fryer. Cook the air fried rice at 360 degrees F for 15 minutes stirring every 5 minutes. Add in the green onion tops during the last minutes of cooking time, stirring them in until well combined.
7. Serve immediately.

Air Fryer Gnocchi With Pesto Dip
Servings: 8
Cooking Time: 10-30 Minutes

Ingredients:
- 2 x 400g packs fresh gnocchi
- 2 tbsp olive oil
- 160g/5⅔oz mayonnaise
- 3 tsp pesto
- salt and freshly ground black pepper

Directions:
1. Preheat the air fryer to 180C. Toss the gnocchi with the oil in a bowl and season well with salt and pepper. Cook in the air fryer for 20 minutes, turning halfway, until crispy and lightly golden.
2. Meanwhile, mix the mayonnaise and pesto together in a small bowl. Serve alongside the gnocchi with some cocktail sticks to skewer the gnocchi for dipping.

Recipe Tips

The pesto dip can be changed for all kinds of interesting dipping sauces. Cajun mayo, honey sriracha, smoky BBQ or hot honey mustard are just a few easy throw-together dips for these easy party snacks.

You can also cook these in a preheated oven at 200C/180C Fan/Gas 6 for 20 minutes, or until golden-brown all over.

Air Fryer Taco Calzones

Servings: 4
Cooking Time: 10 Minutes

Ingredients:
- 1 tube Pillsbury thin crust pizza dough
- 1 cup taco meat
- 1 cup shredded cheddar

Directions:
1. Spread out your sheet of pizza dough on a clean surface. Using a pizza cutter, cut the dough into 4 even squares.
2. Cut each square into a large circle using the pizza cutter. Set the dough scraps aside to make cinnamon sugar bites.
3. Top one half of each circle of dough with 1/4 cup taco meat and 1/4 cup shredded cheese.
4. Fold the empty half over the meat and cheese and press the edges of the dough together with a fork to seal it tightly. Repeat with all four calzones.
5. Gently pick up each calzone and spray it with pan spray or olive oil. Arrange them in your Air Fryer basket.
6. Cook the calzones at 325° for 8-10 minutes. Watch them closely at the 8 minute mark so you don't overcook them.
7. Serve with salsa and sour cream.
8. To make cinnamon sugar bites, cut the scraps of dough into even sized pieces, about 2 inches long. Add them to the Air Fryer basket and cook at 325° for 5 minutes. Immediately toss with 1:4 cinnamon sugar mixture.

Air-fryer White Pizza

Servings: 4
Cooking Time: 6 Minutes

Ingredients:
- 1 recipe Food Processor Pizza Dough
- 2 tablespoon olive oil
- ¾ cup whole milk ricotta cheese
- 1 cup shredded mozzarella cheese (4 oz.)
- 1 teaspoon crushed red pepper
- ½ teaspoon sea salt flakes
- 2 tablespoon chopped fresh basil
- Honey (optional)
- Food Processor Pizza Dough
- Olive oil or nonstick cooking spray
- 2 cup all-purpose flour
- 1 package active dry yeast
- 1 teaspoon sugar
- ½ teaspoon salt
- 1 tablespoon olive oil
- ⅔ cup warm water (105°F to 115°F)

Directions:
1. Preheat air fryer at 375°F. Divide Food Processor Pizza Dough into four 4-oz. portions. On a lightly floured surface, roll one portion of dough into an 8-inch circle. Prick all over with a fork. Place in air-fryer basket and cook 3 minutes. Remove from basket and place, top side down, on work surface.
2. Drizzle crust lightly with 1 1/2 tsp. of the oil and spread with 3 Tbsp. of the ricotta cheese. Sprinkle with 1/4 cup of the mozzarella cheese, 1/4 tsp. of the crushed red pepper, and 1/8 tsp. of the salt. Return

pizza to air-fryer basket and cook 3 to 4 minutes or until cheese is melted and golden. Repeat with remaining dough and toppings.
3. Before serving, sprinkle pizzas with basil and, if desired, drizzle with honey.
4. Food Processor Pizza Dough
5. Coat a medium bowl with nonstick cooking spray; set aside. In a food processor combine flour, yeast, sugar, and salt. With the food processor running, add olive oil and warm water. Process until a dough forms. Remove and shape into a smooth ball. Place dough in the prepared bowl; turn once to coat dough surface. Cover bowl with plastic wrap. Let stand in a warm place until doubled in size (45 to 60 minutes).

*Tip

For a delicious garlic-herb crust, add 1 Tbsp. dried Italian seasoning, crushed, and 2 cloves garlic, minced, to the flour mixture when preparing the dough.

*Make-Ahead Directions:

At this point, the dough portions can be placed in a storage container that has been lightly coated with nonstick cooking spray or brushed with olive oil. Cover and store in the refrigerator for up to 24 hours. Or place each dough portion in a freezer bag that has been lightly coated with nonstick cooking spray or brushed with olive oil. Seal, label, and freeze up to 3 months. Thaw in the refrigerator before using.

Air Fryer Mini Corn Dogs

Servings: 4
Cooking Time: 8 Minutes

Ingredients:
- 20 mini corn dogs frozen
- toppings Ketchup, mustard

Directions:
1. Place the mini corn dogs into the air fryer basket, without stacking or overlapping. If you have a smaller basket, air fry 10 at a time.
2. Air fry at 380 degrees F for 9-11 minutes, or until corn dogs reach your desired crispness and the hot dog in the middle is cooked.
3. Serve with your favorite toppings.

NOTES

I make this recipe in my Cosori 8 qt. air fryer or 6.8 quart air fryer. Depending on your air fryer, size and wattages, cooking time may need to be adjusted 1-2 minutes.

Air Fryer Pizza

Servings: 2

Ingredients:
- 2 (8-oz.) packages pizza dough
- 1 tbsp. extra virgin olive oil, divided
- 1/3 c. crushed tomatoes
- 1 clove garlic, minced
- 1/2 tsp. oregano
- Kosher salt
- Freshly ground black pepper
- 1/2 (8-oz.) mozzarella ball, cut into ¼" slices
- Basil leaves, for serving

Directions:
1. On a clean, floured surface, gently flatten ball of dough with your hands until about 8" in diameter (or roughly smaller than your air fryer basket). Repeat with second dough ball. Brush both with olive oil and transfer one, oil side up, into the basket of your air fryer.
2. In a medium bowl, stir to combine crushed tomatoes, garlic, and oregano, and season with salt and pepper. Spoon half tomato mixture onto the center of rolled out pizza dough, then spread into an even layer, leaving ½" outer crust bare.
3. Add half the mozzarella slices to pizza. Air fry on 400° for 10 to 12 minutes, or until crust is golden and cheese is melted.
4. Remove first pizza from air fryer basket using 2 pairs of tongs, and garnish with basil leaves. Assemble and cook second pizza, garnish, and serve.

Air Fryer Grilled Cheese And Ham Crescent Pockets

Servings: 4

Ingredients:
- 1 can (8 oz) refrigerated Pillsbury™ Original Crescent Rolls (8 Count) or 1 can (8 oz) refrigerated Pillsbury™ Original Crescent Dough Sheet
- 4 slices (0.8 oz each) Swiss cheese, cut in half (from 7-oz package)
- 4 slices (4 oz) cooked deli ham (from 7-oz package)

Directions:
1. Cut two 8-inch rounds of cooking parchment paper. Place round in bottom of air fryer basket. Spray with cooking spray.
2. If using crescent rolls, separate dough into 4 rectangles; reshape each rectangle to form 6x4-inch rectangle, firmly pressing perforations to seal; if using dough sheet, unroll and cut into 4 (6x4-inch) rectangles.
3. Place one cheese slice half on center of each rectangle to within 1/2 inch of edge. Top each with 1 slice ham (folding in half to fit), and top with another cheese slice half. Fold dough from top over cheese and ham; firmly press edges with fork to seal. Place two filled crescents onto parchment round in basket of air fryer, spacing apart.
4. Set air fryer to 325°F; bake 8 to 10 minutes or until deep golden brown on top and sturdy enough to turn over with tongs. With tongs or spatula, carefully turn over crescents, and bake 3 to 6 minutes longer or until dough is deep golden brown and thoroughly cooked. Cover loosely with foil to keep warm while baking second batch. Repeat for remaining filled crescents, and place on remaining parchment round in basket of air fryer. Bake as directed as above.

Air Fryer Pita Pizzas

Servings: 1
Cooking Time: 10 Minutes

Ingredients:
- 1 pita bread
- 2 Tablespoons (30 ml) pizza sauce or tomato sauce
- 1/4 cup (28 g) shredded cheese
- salt , to taste
- black pepper , to taste
- OPTIONAL TOPPINGS
- Pepperoni, cooked Sausage, Bacon pieces, diced Ham, sliced or diced Tomatoes, Mushrooms, Pineapple, etc.
- OTHER SAUCE OPTIONS
- BBQ Sauce, Salsa, White (Alfredo) Sauce, Pesto, etc.
- EQUIPMENT
- Air Fryer
- Air Fryer Rack optional

Directions:
1. Place the pita in air fryer (if making multiple pita pizzas, make sure it is in just a single layer - cook in batches if needed). Air Fry at 360°F/182°C for 2 minutes.
2. Flip the pita bread over. Continue to Air fry at 360°F/182°C for another 1-2 minutes (if you want the crust extra crispy - air fry each side a couple minutes more).
3. Spread the sauce over the toasted pita bread. Top with cheese and add additional salt, pepper and other preferred toppings.
4. To keep your topping from flying around, place an air fryer rack over the pita pizzas.
5. Air Fry the pizzas at 360°F/182°C for 2-5 minutes or until heated through and cheese is melted. Allow to cool for a couple minutes, then slice and serve warm.

Air Fryer Elote

Servings: 4
Cooking Time: 10 Minutes

Ingredients:
- Corn
- 4 ears of corn on the cob shucked and cleaned
- 2 tablespoons olive oil separated
- 1/2 teaspoon salt separated
- 1/2 teaspoon ground black pepper
- Elote Sauce
- ½ cup plain Greek yogurt
- 2 tablespoons mayo
- 2 oz. cotija cheese crumbled
- 1 tablespoon fresh lime juice
- 1 tablespoon lime zest
- ¼ teaspoon cayenne pepper

Directions:
1. Preheat the air fryer to 350°F. Drizzle the 4 ears of corn with 1 tablespoon of olive oil. Massage the oil into the corn with your hands. Season the corn with ½ teaspoon of salt and ½ teaspoon of pepper.
2. Add 1 tablespoon of olive oil to the bottom of the air fryer and then transfer the corn to the air fryer. Cook the corn for 10 minutes, flipping halfway.
3. While the corn is cooking, add all of the ingredients (except for the cayenne pepper) for the elote sauce to a bowl and mix to combine. Pour the sauce on a large plate. Spread the sauce out evenly.
4. Remove the corn from the air fryer and roll each ear of corn in the elote sauce. Use a spoon to drizzle more elote sauce over the corn. Then season the corn with the cayenne pepper. Enjoy!
5. Air fryer elote on a plate.

Tips & Notes

Every air fryer is different, so the cook time may vary slightly.

If cayenne pepper is too spicy, replace it with ground paprika.

Air Fryer French Bread Pizzas

Servings: 2
Cooking Time: 10 Minutes

Ingredients:
- 1 French bread loaf
- 1/2 cup (120 ml) pizza sauce or tomato sauce
- 1/3 cup (40 g) shredded cheese
- salt , to taste
- black pepper , to taste
- OPTIONAL TOPPINGS
- Pepperoni, cooked Sausage, Bacon pieces, diced Ham, sliced or diced Tomatoes, Mushrooms, Pineapple, etc.
- OTHER SAUCE OPTIONS
- BBQ Sauce, Salsa, White (Alfredo) Sauce, Pesto, etc.
- EQUIPMENT
- Air Fryer
- Air Fryer Rack optional

Directions:
1. Cut French bread loaf to fit the length of your air fryer. Slice in half lengthwise.
2. Lightly spray both sides for an extra crispy crust. Place in air fryer basket/tray with the bottom (crust) side up (only cook in a single layer - cook the pizzas in batches if needed). Air Fry at 360°F/182°C about 2 minutes.
3. Flip the bread, add sauce & toppings.
4. Cover toppings with an air fryer rack to keep toppings from flying around.
5. Air Fry 360°F/182°C for 2-4 minutes or until heated through and cheese is melted. Try air frying for about 2 minutes first. If you want the top to be crispier, add additional minute or two until the pizza is crispy and cheese is melted.
6. Allow pizza to cool for about 2 minutes. Serve warm.

Air Fryer Hot Pockets

Servings: 1
Cooking Time: 12 Minutes

Ingredients:
- 1 Frozen Hot Pocket
- EQUIPMENT
- Air Fryer

Directions:
1. Place the frozen hot pocket in the air fryer basket. If cooking multiple hot pockets, spread out into a single even layer. No oil spray is needed.
2. Air Fry at 380°F/193°C for 10 minutes. If needed, flip the hot pocket over and cook for another 1-3 minutes or until cooked to your preference. Cooking more than 1 hot pocket at a time might require more cooking time.

NOTES
Air Frying Tips and Notes:
No Oil Necessary. Cook Frozen - Do not thaw first.
Shake or turn if needed. Don't overcrowd the air fryer basket.
Recipe timing is based on a non-preheated air fryer. If cooking in multiple batches of hot pockets back to back, the following batches may cook a little quicker.
Recipes were tested in 3.7 to 6 qt. air fryers. If using a larger air fryer, the hot pockets might cook quicker so adjust cooking time.

Air Fryer Nuts And Bolts

Servings: 4
Cooking Time: 25 Minutes

Ingredients:
- 2 cups dried farfalle pasta
- 60ml (1/4 cup) extra virgin olive oil
- 2 tbsp brown sugar
- 2 tsp smoked paprika
- 1 tsp onion powder
- 1/2 tsp garlic powder
- 1/2 tsp chilli powder
- 1 cup pretzels
- 80g (1/2 cup) raw macadamias
- 80g (1/2 cup) raw cashews
- 1 cup Kellog's Nutri-grain cereal
- 1 tsp sea salt
- Select all ingredients

Directions:
1. Cook pasta in a large saucepan of boiling salted water until just tender. Drain well. Transfer to a tray. Pat dry with paper towel. Transfer to a large bowl.
2. Combine oil, sugar, paprika, onion, garlic and chilli powders in a small bowl. Spoon half of the mixture over pasta. Toss to coat.
3. Preheat air fryer on 200C. Place pasta in air fryer basket. Cook for 5 minutes. Shake basket. Cook for a further 5-6 minutes or until golden and crisp. Transfer to a large bowl.
4. Place pretzels and nuts in a bowl. Add remaining spice mixture. Toss to coat. Place in air fryer basket. Cook on 180C for 3 minutes. Shake basket. Cook for a further 2-3 minutes or until golden. Add to pasta, then add cereal. Sprinkle with salt. Toss to combine. Cool completely. Serve.

Char Siu Dinner

Servings: 5

Ingredients:
- Marinade:
- 1 teaspoon five-spice powder
- 2 teaspoons kosher salt
- ¼ teaspoon ground white pepper
- 4 tablespoons granulated sugar
- 1½ tablespoons soy sauce
- 2 tablespoons hoisin sauce
- 1 tablespoon Chinese rice wine
- 2 tablespoons honey
- 2 garlic cloves, minced
- 2 cubes red fermented bean curd, mashed
- 3 teaspoons red fermented bean curd liquid
- Pork:
- 2 pounds Boston butt (pork shoulder), tops and sides scored
- 3 tablespoons honey

- Oil spray
- For Serving:
- 2 cups short grain white rice, steamed
- 1 cup Taiwanese cabbage, sauteed, for serving
- Items Needed:
- Pastry brush

Directions:
1. Combine marinade ingredients in a large bowl and mix until well combined. Set 4 tablespoons of marinade aside in the refrigerator.
2. Remove the thick, fatty pork rinds from around the entire piece of pork shoulder.
3. Slice the pork into smaller pieces, about 2-cm long and ¾-inch thick.
4. Place the pork and marinade into a large resealable plastic bag and shake until fully coated. Marinate for 1-2 days in the refrigerator.
5. Rest the pork for 30 minutes at room temperature before cooking.
6. Select the Preheat function on the Air Fryer, adjust temperature to 400°F, and press Start/Pause.
7. Mix the honey, 1½ tablespoons of water, and the 4 tablespoons of reserved marinade in a small bowl to make a basting mixture.
8. Spray the inner basket of the air fryer with oil spray.
9. Brush both sides of the pork slices with the basting mixture, then place into the preheated air fryer.

Note: The pieces pork can be touching each other, but should not be stacked on top of each other. You may need to work in batches. Set temperature to 400°F and time to 12 minutes, press Shake, then press Start/Pause.

Flip the pork pieces over and brush more of the basting mixture on each side halfway through cooking. The Shake Reminder will let you know when.

Remove the pork when done, then transfer to a wire rack.

Baste the top of the pork with the remaining basting mixture.

Serve the Char Siu over steamed white rice with a side of sautéed Taiwanese cabbage.

Air Fryer Spaghetti Squash
Servings: 4
Cooking Time: 35 Minutes

Ingredients:
- 1 medium spaghetti squash about 3 pounds
- 1 tablespoon olive oil
- ½ teaspoon kosher salt
- ¼ teaspoon black pepper

Directions:
1. Preheat the air fryer to 370°F.
2. Cut the spaghetti squash in half lengthwise. Scoop out the seeds and discard (or save for roasting).
3. Brush the cut side of the squash with oil and season with salt & pepper.
4. Place cut side up in the air fryer and cook 25-30 minutes or until tender and the strands separate easily with a fork.
5. Once cooked, run a fork along the strands of the squash to separate.
6. Toss with butter if desired or season with additional salt and pepper.

Notes
Spaghetti squash seeds can be saved and cooked like pumpkin seeds.

Cook time can vary slightly based on the size of the squash.

Once the strands are separated, they can be topped with your favorite meat sauce and placed back into the squash shells. Top them with mozzarella cheese and air fryer until browned and bubbly.

Keep leftovers in the fridge for up to 3 days. Freeze leftovers in zippered bags for up to 6 months. Let thaw at room temperature before using.

Air Fryer Tostones
Servings: 2
Cooking Time: 20 Minutes

Ingredients:
- 1 large green plantain (ends trimmed and peeled (6 oz after))
- olive oil spray (I like Bertolli)
- 1 cup water
- 1 teaspoon kosher salt
- 3/4 teaspoon garlic powder

Directions:
1. With a sharp knife cut a slit along the length of the plantain skin, this will make it easier to peel. Cut the plantain into 1 inch pieces, 8 total.
2. In a small bowl combine the water with salt and garlic powder.
3. Preheat the air fryer to 400F.
4. When ready, spritz the plantain with olive oil and cook 6 minutes, you might have to do this in 2 batches.
5. Remove from the air fryer and while they are hot mash them with a tostonera or the bottom of a jar or measuring cup to flatten.
6. Dip them in the seasoned water and set aside.
7. Preheat the air fryer to 400F once again and cook, in batches 5 minutes on each side, spraying both sides of the plantains with olive oil.
8. When done, give them another spritz of oil and season with salt. Eat right away.

Buttermilk Ranch Dressing
Servings: 16

Ingredients:
- 1 cup buttermilk
- ⅔ cup mayonnaise (I use low fat)
- ⅔ cup sour cream (I use low fat)
- 1 tablespoon fresh chives chopped
- 1 tablespoon fresh dill chopped
- 1 tablespoon fresh parsley chopped
- ¾ teaspoon garlic powder
- ¾ teaspoon onion powder
- ½ teaspoon salt & pepper (each)

Directions:
1. Mix all ingredients in a bowl.
2. Refrigerate at least 30 minutes before serving.

Notes
Reduce buttermilk to ¾ cup to make ranch dip.
If using dried herbs, use 1 teaspoon of each (instead of 1 tablespoon).
Keeps 1 week in the fridge.

Air Fryer Reheating Leftover Pizza
Servings: 1
Cooking Time: 6 Minutes

Ingredients:
- 1-2 slices leftover pizza
- oil spray , (optional to lightly coat the pizza so toppings don't dry out - need depends on yoout particular toppings)
- EQUIPMENT
- Air Fryer

Directions:
1. Place foil or perforated parchment sheet to base on air fryer basket, rack or tray. Place the pizza on top. If needed, lightly spray the top of pizza so that the toppings don't burn or dry out (optional).
2. Air Fry at 360°F/180°C for 3-6 minutes or until cooked to your desired crispness. If unsure, start cooking for 3 minutes first. Then check to see if it's to your liking. Cook additional minute or two if you want the pizza to be crispier. Deep dish crusts will take a little longer, while thin crust will be slightly quicker.
3. Let the slice of pizza cool for a touch & enjoy!

Air Frying Tips and Notes:
Recipe timing is based on a non-preheated air fryer. If cooking in multiple slices back to back, the following slices may cook a little quicker because the air fryer is already hot.
Recipes were tested in 3.7 to 6 qt. air fryers. If using a larger air fryer, the pizza slices might cook quicker so adjust cooking time.

Air Fryer Sausages

Servings: 8
Cooking Time: 10 Minutes

Ingredients:
- 8 sausages

Directions:
1. Preheat the air fryer to 180C (350F)
2. Pierce each sausage with a knife or fork.
3. Lay sausages in the air fryer basket.
4. Cook for 10 minutes, checking on them and turning them over after 5 minutes.

Notes
Use any sausages you want to - any flavour and any size. For smaller sausages check on them before 10 minutes as they will cook in a quicker time.

Air Fryer Bratwurst

Servings: 5
Cooking Time: 15 Minutes

Ingredients:
- 1 pound uncooked bratwurst
- 5 hoagie rolls optional
- toppings for serving dijon mustard, sauerkraut, pickles, etc

Directions:
1. Preheat the air fryer to 360°F.
2. Place the brats in a single layer in the air fryer basket.
3. Cook them for 8 minutes, then flip and cook for an additional 5-6 minutes or until they reach an internal temperature of 165°F.
4. Serve in rolls and/or with desired toppings.

Notes
Ensure brats reach an internal temperature of 165°F.
Do not pierce the brats before cooking or they will lose their juices. Use caution when checking the temperature, they can squirt hot liquid when pierced.
Allow brats to cool for a few minutes before serving or topping.

Air Fryer Corn Dogs

Servings: 5
Cooking Time: 9 Minutes

Ingredients:
- 5 Corn Dogs

Directions:
1. How To Make Regular Sized Frozen Corn Dogs in the Air Fryer
2. Preheat Air Fryer to 380 degrees Fahrenheit. Prepare the Air Fryer basket with olive oil cooking spray or parchment paper.
3. Place the corn dogs in Air Fryer Basket.
4. Set the cook time to 9 minutes. After 5 minutes, flip the corn dogs in the Air Fryer Basket and then cook for the remainder of time.
5. Serve with your favorite condiments and side items.
6. How To Make Mini Sized Frozen Corn Dogs in the Air Fryer
7. Preheat Air Fryer to 380 degrees Fahrenheit. Prepare the basket with cooking spray or parchment paper.
8. Place the corn dogs in preheated Air Fryer Basket. Be sure to line them up in a single layer.
9. Set the cooking time to 7 minutes. After 4 minutes, flip the mini corn dogs and cook for the remainder of the time.
10. Serve with your favorite condiments or side items.

NOTES
It is best to preheat the Air Fryer before making any of your recipes, including frozen corn dogs. If you're not preheating the Air Fryer cook time will be different. You won't get the same results and your foods may not be cooked thoroughly through.
Just as you would preheat the oven, you want to preheat the Air Fryer as well so that you can ensure you have fully cooked food and that you are also using the correct cook time.

Air Fryer Sausage Rolls

Servings: 12
Cooking Time: 10 Minutes

Ingredients:
- Air Fryer Sausage Rolls
- 3 sausages Note 1
- 3 sheets puff pastry
- 1 tbsp sesame seeds
- 1 eggs

Directions:
1. Air Fryer Sausage Rolls
2. Turn the air fryer on to 180°C/350 F for 15 mins
3. Use a knife and chopping board to remove the casing from the sausages
4. Add egg to a small bowl, pierce yoke and whisk
5. Place a sheet of puff pastry (thawed) onto the chopping board and place 1 off the sausages on top
6. Roll the pastry around the sausage, then use a pastry brush to coat the top of the pastry where the 2 bits of pastry will meet
7. Continue to roll the pastry around the sausage and again brush one side of where the pastry joins with the egg
8. Repeat for each sausage
9. Brush the top of the length of the long rolled sausage with egg
10. Sprinkle the top with sesame seeds
11. Use a knife to cut the excess pastry off each end
12. Then cut the long sausage roll into 4 smaller rolls
13. Spray the Air Fryer Basket with oil (or use baking paper) then place raw sausage rolls into Air Fryer (work in batches)
14. Cook sausage rolls in Air Fryer for 7- 9 mins until pastry is golden and crispy
15. Serve with sauce

Air Fryer Chili Cheese Dogs

Servings: 2
Cooking Time: 5 Minutes

Ingredients:
- 2 hot dogs
- 2 sausage rolls
- 1/2 cup canned or homemade chili of choice warmed or at room temperature
- 1/2 cup shredded cheddar cheese*

Directions:
1. Preheat your air fryer to 400 degrees.
2. Place the hot dogs inside the air fryer and cook for 4 minutes, turning halfway through.
3. Remove the hot dogs from the air fryer and place inside sausage rolls. Gently place each one in the air fryer and add half of the cheddar cheese evenly on top of the hot dogs.
4. Add the chili and then top with the remaining cheddar cheese.
5. Turn air fryer to 350 degrees and cook for 1- 2 minutes until cheese has melted and chili is warm.
6. Carefully remove the chili cheese dogs from the air fryer and enjoy immediately.

NOTES
*Mexican cheese can be substituted for cheddar cheese
If cooking hot dogs from frozen:
Place small slits on hot dogs using a knife. Cook on 350 (preheated) for 7-8 minutes until hot dog is heated thoroughly.

Printed in Great Britain
by Amazon